AF207058

Confused Girl

GIOVANNA SILVESTRE

Confused Girl

FIND YOUR PEACE IN THE CHAOS

BLACK STONE PUBLISHING

This book is lovingly dedicated to my late father, Giuseppe Silvestre, who passed away during its publication. His unwavering belief in me and his constant encouragement to follow my heart, even in the face of uncertainty, have been my guiding lights. His trust, even when I embarked on a two-year solo journey around the world to write this book, a venture that filled him with apprehension, was a testament to his faith in my abilities. My father instilled in me the tenacity to never give up and to fearlessly chase my dreams. This invaluable lesson paved the way for the creation of the words you're about to read.

CONFUSED GIRL

FIND YOUR PEACE IN THE CHAOS

is also a tribute to all you Confused Girls out there, embarking on your own journeys of self-discovery. If you're reading this, you've already opened the door and taken the first step in revealing your true self.

I am deeply honored to share my experiences and insights with you. May this book be your guide through the labyrinth of confusion, and may it illuminate your path toward the awe-inspiring breakthroughs that await.

CONTENTS

Confusion Is a Virtue

> What is important is to spread confusion, not
> eliminate it.
>
> —Salvador Dalí

I want to acknowledge that you may be reading this book because you're feeling confused about something in your life. If that's the case, get ready to celebrate this profound moment. You are on the verge of a significant breakthrough that, from this day forward, can change your life.

You might also be thinking: *What is this lady talking about?*

Who could possibly be excited and positive about being confused?

The answer is *me*.

Why do I consider confusion a gift? Because confusion holds the seed for transformation and illumination. Nothing grows or is revealed through stagnation. Confusion is the opposite of standing in place. It is the condition of feeling bewildered or uncertain. When you're confused, you're mystified, perplexed, and confounded. You're in motion, searching for the truth, for the way in or out. When you're confused, you're on the hunt for answers. Confusion is juicy.

For all these reasons, I say, "Yay for being a Confused Girl!"

Okay, I confess, I haven't always felt this way. Just a few years ago, I wasn't so excited about being a Confused Girl. Back then, I didn't understand that confusion is a virtue. But now I know, in an *ah-ha* kind of way, that confusion is what the Divine uses so we can see the world from a fuller perspective. This newfound outlook guided me toward a breakthrough, and it can lead you there too.

I learned there's no reason to feel ashamed when you don't have all the answers. It can be liberating just to sit in your confusion, luxuriating on the metaphorical cushion of the unknown. You can sense in the midst of your cloud of bewilderment that something is going to happen. The sun is about to break through.

Of course, you don't always want to be confused any more than you want to be a Know-It-All, or as I like to say, a KIA. (Let's admit, no one really likes a KIA, and honestly, in today's complex world, it's impossible to know everything. So, why pretend that you know it all?) But confusion is a natural by-product of growth. It encourages us to emerge from internal or external upheaval with greater self-confidence and a stronger sense of purpose. We all go through different phases in our lives, and every chapter is in service of our greater good. Without going through a state of confusion, we might never see the bright light of awareness.

One area of our lives that sparks considerable perplexity is our professions. After all, it's where we spend approximately a third of our existence. According to a Gallup poll reported by CNBC in 2022, career unhappiness is at an all-time high: 50 percent of workers said they feel stressed out at their jobs every day, 41 percent said they're worried, 22 percent are sad, and 18 percent are angry.[1] This dissatisfaction, along with the increase of technology in our lives, has contributed to traditional career paths and job security being thrown to the wind. We find ourselves at a crossroads where flexibility and the gig economy appear to be the new frontier for the Gen Zers among us. With this newfound job freedom comes a mix of opportunity and excitement, along with an overwhelming array of choices, uncertainty, and a departure from the old ways of doing things.

The rapid push of technology has not only revolutionized industries but created a breathless urgency to keep adapting. Today's careers are a labyrinth of options, with new job titles flying by faster than shooting stars. The pressure to find passion and purpose in our work has intensified as societal expectations and personal aspirations collide. We're left with these crucial questions: What truly brings you joy and satisfaction? If you're not following the path that's been paved, then what path are you creating?

To answer these questions, you have to know yourself and your desires, and this book can help.

The world as we know it is undergoing a seismic shift. But this shift isn't just about how we earn our living. It's about redefining what truly matters to us. We're reevaluating our priorities, choosing to focus more on the aspects of life that fuel our soul rather than just our bank accounts or other people's expectations of us.

We have more choices than ever. This shift has brought forth a myriad of new opportunities in various aspects of life, such as education, entertainment, travel, and social connections. The positive side of this shift is that we now have more freedom and agency to pursue our passions, access a wealth of knowledge, connect with diverse individuals globally, and create meaningful experiences. However, there are also negative consequences, such as information overload, the pressure to constantly chase the new (FOMO?), and the risk of losing genuine human connection in an increasingly digital world. Don't get me started on the subject of online dating! The way we meet and interact with people has dramatically changed since the birth of the smartphone, and not necessarily for the better. I'm not telling you anything you don't already know (or haven't experienced) when I say online dating is the enemy of self-esteem. If someone ghosts us, we're likely to either drown in self-pity or be comforted by thoughts of revenge.

Also, in the Western world, the role of women has changed immensely. We are not all expected to get married and have babies, which raises even more questions about who we are and what we want out of life. Do you want to be a wife? Do you want to have kids? Do you want to be single? Do you want to concentrate on your career? Do you want to travel and have adventures?

With these new doors opening comes the inevitable byproduct: confusion. When you're trying to create your own unique version of life, one where you mix and match different elements to fit your ideals, confusion is bound to crop up. It's part of the package, an unavoidable pit stop. Deep down inside, we are all Confused Girls. Yes, you read that right—each of us, from every corner of the world, is grappling with some sort of confusion. It could be about our health, our finances, our career, our love life, our family ties, or even our very purpose in life.

It could be that you are depressed at this moment, feeling nothing except numbness. Alternatively, you may be tormented inside, unable to get past your shame. I've been there, and I understand. Maybe you are at a loss on how to escape this state of being. It can be incredibly challenging to find a way forward when you feel trapped in these emotions. However, it's important to remember there is hope and you are holding it in your hands.

In this book, I will share my journey out of depression, detailing how I took a leap of faith by breaking away from the entertainment industry and my family business. Choosing to follow my heart, I launched my own blog, which ultimately led to the creation of an activewear line, global travel experiences, and the completion of this very book. Most importantly, through this process, I discovered my true self and achieved a deep spiritual alignment with my soul.

Throughout these chapters, I'll delve into the various learning moments that have shaped my life—from nurturing creativity and cultivating self-love to prioritizing health, relationships, and more. Prepare to be captivated as we uncover the secrets to avoiding joy destroyers and releasing the heavy burden of guilt and shame. Imagine a life free from the weight of nagging doubts and insecurities. Together, we will explore the pitfalls of comparisons, unraveling their positive potential and changing them into stepping stones rather than stumbling blocks.

We will unleash the creative goddess within you, for you are the embodiment of creativity itself. Yes, you are a Goddess of Creativity, and I will show you how to harness your creative genius, allowing it to radiate into every aspect of your existence. As we embark on this adventure of self-discovery, you will learn the art of loving the heck out of yourself. Self-love is not just a fleeting trend; it is the foundation upon which your extraordinary life will be built.

And when it comes to relationships, we will unlock the secrets of decoding them, enabling you to understand and revitalize your connections with others in ways you never thought possible. You will learn to clear out emotional messes (and physical ones), creating space for what truly matters and igniting a sense of profound clarity and purpose.

After reading this book, you will be able to summon the courage and confidence needed to manifest your wildest dreams. But that's just the beginning. Destiny is not a fixed point; it's a moving target, and I will guide you on how to adapt and flourish, no matter where your path leads. Brace yourself for an enchanting exploration of manifesting health and happiness, where you'll acquire the tools to attract the positive vibes and well-being you truly desire. Yes, my friend, you are destined for greatness, and by the end of these pages, you will be equipped with the unwavering power and resilience to conquer any obstacle that life throws your way.

So, take a deep breath. Discovering and charting a new course requires introspection, self-discovery, an ability to make changes, and a willingness to open our hearts and accept what is inevitable . . . confusion. Accept where you're at and unleash any shackles of shame that are holding you back. Let your authenticity and personal truth be your driving force. Ladies, you are on a journey to uncover your true nature. You are a warrior, a force to be reckoned with. You can make a difference in this world. You—right here and right now.

If you feel lost, I promise you are in good company. We're all in this together, navigating a whirlwind of change, trying to figure out our own unique paths. As you will discover in this book, the first step every Confused Girl must take is to surrender to her confusion.

But first, I want to share my journey and let you know how this girl learned to embrace her confusion.

CHAPTER 1

Little Miss Confused

> We cannot change what we are not aware of, and once we are aware, we cannot help but change.
>
> —Sheryl Sandberg

During the bewildering and complicated years of my late twenties, I confessed a dark truth to Anna, my closest and most trusted friend. In a matter-of-fact way, as if I were reporting the weather, I told her, "I hate my life." It was a jarring news flash, considering everything around us seemed storybook perfect.

We were having dinner in the Lido Restaurant at Shell Beach on the Central Coast of California. The sun was setting over the Pacific Ocean, turning the sky the color of blood orange. Our food was so fresh it practically held its own conversation. And Anna, in her vintage jeans, blazer, and diamond tennis necklace, was a model of West Coast elegance.

She fixed her eyes on me.

"Anna, I just feel so empty," I said in a whisper.

My friend's face dropped like a stone. We sat in silence for a few long minutes until Anna twisted a strand of corn-silk hair behind her ear and finally spoke. "I don't get it," she said. "I always thought you, of all people, had it totally together."

She went on in a rush. "Oh my God, it's completely unexpected. You're supposed to be the upbeat, positive person. What the *fah* is happening?"

Anna's observation was spot-on.

To the rest of the world, I was happy-go-lucky, full of can-do energy, and always ready to flash my thousand-watt smile. But secretly, I was uncomfortable in my own skin. Lately, I had felt untethered, pulled here and there by a barrage of wildly negative thoughts. I had spent years working in the entertainment industry and then at my family's restaurant business, but I hadn't felt fulfilled in either. And then, to top it off, I had broken up with my boyfriend and was working small gigs to survive. It had been a rough ride, to say the least. I was just trying to figure out who I was and what I really wanted to do with my life.

I could have opened up to Anna, but misery is like mercury, hard to pin down. Instead, I went into my default mode, took a gulp of rosé, and changed the subject so I wouldn't ruin her dinner.

"Oh, it's nothing." I waved my hand in the air and pretended it was a passing mood I had successfully shooed into the warm breeze. My game face took over, and I quickly changed the conversation to a happier time.

"Hey, remember our junior year in high school when we

drove around town while Ashley mooned everyone and you took pics of their reactions?" *And just like that*, as Carrie Bradshaw might say, the moment of my truth and authenticity passed like our basket of bread.

Though not for long. The problem with using people-pleasing as a Band-Aid is, eventually, all coping methods run their course. Over the following weeks, I fell deeper into a well of despair, ruminating over my conversation with Anna and regretting what was left unsaid. It felt like a prelude for what was to come, and sure enough, eventually I could no longer mask my sinking sadness.

A few months later, I found myself in Park City, Utah, at the swank Sundance Film Festival, where independent movies are screened to win recognition among industry elites that might gain them a big distribution deal or a fast track to the Academy Awards. It's a whirling vortex of networking, deal-making, collaborating, and dressing in casual yet exorbitantly expensive clothes—a rarefied experience where people pretend not to ogle the likes of Robert Redford, Steven Spielberg, and Sofia Coppola.

I was twenty-nine and out of work. My Hollywood friends had invited me to the festival, which seemed like an especially good idea since I was considering returning to the entertainment industry. Although, I had complicated feelings about it based on my past jobs. Trauma, I guess, gets buried. I assumed I would feel confident among the glitzy crowd as I always did when I worked in the film industry . . . but you know what they say about assumptions.

Here I was, attending a private party held in a sprawling mansion that seemed to hang precariously over the Deer Valley cliffs. It was 2014, and the usual wafer-thin celebrities were there, gripping their drinks and milling around.

I was sipping my Diva vodka martini and mingling with some of the most beautiful and successful folks in the world. Yet, all the while, I couldn't stop an avalanche of negative thoughts from free-falling, one on top of the next.

They don't know that you're a fake. You don't even have a real job.

You don't fit in here. You're in a room full of accomplished people, and you have accomplished nothing worthwhile.

Wait until you fall on your face in front of everyone.

You're such a loser.

No wonder no one loves you.

There was no getting that voice to shut up. In this moment, while I was in terror of being exposed for who I really was— nothing—I was also wondering: *Can I be the only one here feeling this way?*

Did it matter? No. I barely had enough energy to hold myself together.

Rather than look like a fool, I took refuge in a deserted hallway outside the kitchen until I could leave the party without revealing that I was falling apart.

When I got back to my room that night, I lay in bed emotionally exhausted with the indisputable understanding that I couldn't go on this way. I could no longer fake it. I was drained; I was lost. To my friends and family, my social media might have painted a picture of a glamorous lifestyle with Hollywood connections and fancy parties and events, but the reality was far from the truth—I was miserable. I was sick of pretending to be happy.

It wasn't the first time I'd found myself horizontal and crying my eyes out; it had become a daily afternoon practice on my kitchen floor. But this night was a whole new level of revelation. My body was shaking like an earthquake. While holding on to the blanket in a panic, I heard an impatient inner voice. It growled: *You have to stop all this bullshit once and for all! Whatever you have to go through to be real again, you've got to do it. Save your soul!*

I was suddenly infused with the understanding that I would have to be ruthlessly devoted to myself—and to change. My body broke out in a feverish sweat.

Through my sobs, I cried out loud, *Please, help me.* I was begging for salvation.

At that point, I had no idea this was going to be an inside job, my personal do-or-die work. It wasn't just about making a quick change in my career. I would have to take a hard, honest look at my past, at what had brought me to this miserable, unfulfilled, empty point in my life. To survive, I had to confront how I had let my life be controlled by ego, instead of focusing on what truly mattered—my soul.

The ego is a complex aspect of our psyche and spirituality. According to *Merriam-Webster*, the ego is defined as "the self especially as contrasted with another self or the world."[2] Wayne Dyer, a renowned self-help author, often used the phrase "Edging God Out" to describe how ego's self-centeredness can separate us from spiritual connection. By prioritizing the ego over spiritual humility and connection to a higher power, we experience a sense of separation and lack of fulfillment.

As the American spiritual leader Ram Dass tells us: "Souls love. That's what souls do. Egos don't, but souls do. Become a soul, look around, and you'll be amazed—all the beings around you are souls. Be one, see one."[3]

This was to be my journey.

%

Looking back on my life, I know I was dealt a hand flush with luck and privilege. My education, which included Mission College Preparatory Catholic High School and the University of Southern California, where I earned a degree in international relations and a minor in global business, gave me a strong foundation for success. (Little did I know, I would start my own global business a decade later. When we look back after enough time, the dots do connect). Both institutions were, and still are, elite private schools devoted to their students' individual needs and strengths. They primed me to wholly believe in myself and reach for my dreams with confidence.

It worked. My first job after college was this Confused Girl's holy grail. I was only twenty-three when I landed a gig in the television industry as a production assistant on a major network reality show. I was thrilled.

The position was supposed to be temporary, but fate had other plans. After only three days, a producer promoted me to post-production coordinator. *OMG*, I had no idea what that even meant, but I picked up skills fast. Within seven months, I killed everything from video editing raw footage, working with sound designers to enhance audio, and telling a cohesive visual story with a process called "color grading." Who knew?

But most of my laser-sharp focus at work was devoted to keeping my forty-year-old boss happy and on an even keel. At five-foot-three she was petite, with enough sizzling personality to ignite a skyscraper. She powered her way through the studio on a combination of her hometown Chicago street smarts, non-stop cigarette smoking, handfuls of prescription pills, and a raspy voice that rattled off a dozen nasty put-downs in thirty seconds or less. Let's just call her Put-Down Paula, or PDP.

No one wanted to be on PDP's bad side, least of all me. That's why during my twelve-to-fourteen-hour workdays, I spent most of my time sympathizing with her complaints and insults about everyone from the director's burned-out assistant (*moron*) to her sweet mom back in the Windy City (*clueless*). The staff couldn't stand her, and it wasn't long before they slung their grenades of disdain in my direction. If the post-production manager saw me heading his way, his office door slammed like a bomb. I was shunned by colleagues in the kitchen, ignored by the receptionist, and sneered at by production assistants.

By the time I got home, totally spent, usually after 10 p.m., I would tiptoe into my two-bed, two-bath apartment only to end up enduring volcanic annoyance from my roommate, who had a strict "quiet time" policy. No matter how lightly I stepped, shoes off and barely breathing, I was never silent enough, and a tedious lecture inevitably ensued.

I loved our boho-chic place in its prime location, only a few blocks from the beach, but it certainly wasn't a refuge for someone who, at the end of her brutal workday, was dead to the world. Once again, appearances were deceiving. It might have looked like I was living in a dream house, but it was more like a nightmare on Elm Street.

A few months into my reality-show gig, my mother, who was telling all her friends about her "famous Hollywood daughter," visited from our hometown, San Luis Obispo. She wanted to see firsthand what I was doing. My mom, Debby, is a pint-sized woman with a wad of puffy hair and a robust laugh. Despite her cuddly appearance, she isn't the touchy-feely type. Her idea of sharing love and comfort is passing a plate of ravioli.

When she showed up, I did my best to make like I was a big shot—touring the studio, offering snacks from our cafeteria, introducing her to the staff (praying they wouldn't roll their eyes), and strutting with self-importance by throwing my hair back and grinning like a hyena. After I was done leading the grand tour, we left the building, and that's when my Oscar-worthy performance came to a fast finale. Under the blazing sun and oppressive heat, I was battling overwhelming exhaustion, and my facade of carefree competence cracked like an egg. I broke into a stunning torrent of tears, my hands cupping my cheeks and my shoulders folding into themselves.

"I can't take it," I choked.

"Oh, honey, I'm sorry," my mother whispered, giving my shaking body a three-second hug. "Everything is going to be okay."

Then she pulled away and hushed and shushed me until my sobs were silenced into shame.

Why couldn't I just be happy? I knew that every year thousands of young people fresh from college swarm to the West Coast to work in the entertainment industry. I had won the golden ticket, and here I was, a wildfire of emotional pain.

What I really wanted was for my mother to rescue me from my life, from all the fear and anxiety. I wanted her to say something to make it feel like everything was truly going to be okay.

Yet, in this moment, feeling completely alone, I was certain of just one thing: Everything *was not* okay.

Have you ever wished for something to happen, and then when it does, you have regrets? After seven months, my wish came true when the reality show ended—and so did my job. Despite how much I had suffered, I was still enamored with the entertainment industry. *It had to be better somewhere else, right?* I found myself gradually forgetting the excruciating days on that reality show. I was eager to dive back in with renewed determination. I also missed feeling important and believing I was getting somewhere with my career. Oh yeah, I needed a salary as well.

At twenty-four years old, a survivor of reality television propelled by unstoppable chutzpah and a glowing recommendation in hand, I landed a job as the assistant to one of Hollywood's most powerful and feared talent managers. Let's call her Vickie after Queen Victoria, a royal who was smaller than five feet tall, survived several assassination attempts, and had the balls to propose to her husband. Appropriately, Hollywood Vickie's roster included celebrity royals.

I admired Vickie's style. In her early fifties, she was always exquisitely dressed, carrying her petite frame with perfect posture and incredible force. When she slammed her designer bag on the desk each morning, the vibration nearly knocked me off my swivel chair. Still, I managed a cheerful greeting.

"Good morning, Vickie!" I enthusiastically chirped.

"Okay, who called?" was her only response. Flat as concrete.

We shared a big room, so whatever went on during phone calls was privy to both of us. As it turned out, the phone was my nemesis. It was an old-school black landline with buttons at the bottom that lit up when a call came through and flashed when someone was "on hold." I was tethered to that machine.

During my first few days on the job, while learning how to manage the phone system, I mistakenly hung up on dozens of clients, agency assistants, actors, and actor wannabes. But the worst offense was repeatedly disconnecting a major bigwig studio executive.

"How stupid can you be?" he shouted on his third attempt to get to Vickie.

After I finally patched him through, I heard him screaming through the phone, enraged, bad-mouthing me to my new boss. It wasn't a good start.

And it only got worse.

Like a lot of us, I used to be crushed whenever I made a mistake. Clichés like "you're human" and "everyone makes mistakes" never cut it for me. In those days, forgiving myself when I messed up was practically impossible.

And boy, did I mess up.

One of Vickie's A-list celebrity clients (who will remain nameless) was hosting an event that the Queen clearly did not want to attend. "I'm just going to tell her I'm out of town," my boss confided. But on the day of the event, the celebrity phoned the office. I was in the middle of dozens of calamities, and without thinking or even waiting to hear why said celebrity was calling, I said, "Oh, Vickie isn't here. She's shopping downtown with her daughter."

I heard the gasp on the other end of the line.

A few minutes later, my boss called and ripped me a new one.

"What the hell is wrong with you? I told you not to tell

anyone where I was . . . I told her I was out of town . . . and you KNEW. Why would you do this?"

"I'm so, so, so sorry, Vicki. I feel stupid."

"Well, you should. You ARE . . ."

Then the Queen hung up on me.

At this time in my life, it felt like the end of the world. I hadn't toughened up yet. In the entertainment industry, you're expected to develop emotional calluses. One minute, you're the recipient of a barrage of cheek kissing and compliments—"Dahlink, I love you" and "You're a rock star!" The next, you're humiliated and called an idiot.

My fear and anxiety were immense—they had doubled from my first job—and the world felt like it was crashing in on itself. My stomach was doing somersaults, my heart was palpitating, my nights were sleepless, and my skin was erupting zits. I turned to a shrink, hoping I could get a prescription to cure my anxiety. She was sympathetic, and I swear she teared up behind her mega glasses, but she told me that the pills were not to be had without a comprehensive psychological exam. Since I had neither the time nor the money to go that route, I left empty-handed.

There were some glimmers of light through my dark days at the agency. One of my triumphs was orchestrating a deal between one of the agency's celebrity clients and a major shoe company. In fairness, my boss was honorable and gave me full credit for clinching the deal. A minor triumph, but no less satisfying, was that I became a pro at managing the phone. I had conquered my nemesis. And though dealing with Vickie could still get under my skin, I had learned to handle it without letting it crush me. She even offered me a step up as a junior talent manager, acknowledging that I had been her top assistant.

When my one-year commitment was over, I wanted to high-tail it out of there. I felt it was time to move on from her office. I was done with that pressure-cooker environment. I craved working for someone creative, someone who exuded a sense of calmness, and I wanted to be part of a major production. I was seeking a new adventure that promised more creativity and less stress. And, in another act of generosity, Vickie helped arrange an enviable job for me. I was twenty-five years old and would be the personal assistant for a world-renowned director on a popular superhero film for a major production company. It felt as if I had just been given the privilege of planting a flag on the moon.

One of my first big projects was helping the director's wife arrange "an unforgettable birthday bash" for her husband. I was totally game and popping like balloons with ideas.

The event went off without a hitch in their mid-century modern rented home in Manhattan Beach. Most of the partying took place on the deck overlooking the rolling Pacific. Around forty guests were there, and I recall chatting with a distinguished actor, hopelessly trying to match his sophistication.

For a showstopper, my mom baked the director's birthday cake from our family's famous tiramisu recipe. My parents had owned a popular Italian restaurant for thirty years. I grew up working in the restaurant, and our tiramisu was known for being out of this world. On the afternoon of the festivities, I met my mom in Santa Barbara, halfway between San Luis Obispo and LA. We carefully balanced the dessert masterpiece between us, slipped it into the trunk of my car, and prayed I would get to the party without needing to slam on my brakes.

The Silvestre tiramisu was a hit, the party was indeed

unforgettable, and for the first time in a long while, I felt like things were looking up. It seemed like I had finally found my niche in Hollywood, where I could thrive and find happiness. My relationships with the director's family and my colleagues were strong, and I felt at ease at work, able to be myself. It was as if I had shed the heavy weight of anxiety that had plagued me in my previous jobs. There were countless reasons to celebrate that evening, but one dark cloud loomed over it all: the director's first assistant, whom I will call Judas.

Jeans, a button-up flannel shirt, and lime-green tennis shoes made up Judas's daily uniform. His trim, energetic body and clean-cut looks, with a sprinkle of freckles across his nose, gave him an angelic and boyish appearance. But as we've already established, looks can be deceiving. Judas, who had been first assistant to the director for a year before I arrived on the scene, was threatened by the director's wife choosing me as her party partner. It only got worse the closer I became with the filmmaker's family. When snakes feel threatened, they hiss and then attack.

As someone who was also fragile at the time, I understood. Putting myself in Judas's place, I would have been insecure as well. Thinking about it now, I should have sat down with him face-to-face and tried to assure him that I had no intention of stealing his job. But we never had that talk.

Judas went on the defensive. As first assistant, he had many tasks assigned to him, which he was responsible for delegating to other staff. Several times he told higher-ups that he had passed along assignments to me, and they were left undone. In truth, he had never given them to me. I didn't want to come off as whiny or, worse, point blame in his direction, so I remained silent. Once again, I allowed myself to be walked all over. When you do that, there are consequences.

Soon enough, the complaints mounted, rumors whirlpooled, and I was eventually fired. It was nine in the morning, and I had just arrived at the studio when Judas called me over. With his clipboard in hand, he commanded me to "take your things and leave." He added a lot of other stuff about my poor performance, my knack for wasting time, and how I was no longer worth my salary. His final insincerity was: "I'm sorry to see you go." In shock, I said nothing.

In my mind, this was an overwhelming failure. Even though I knew I was unjustly fired, the reality that I had let it happen made it feel like my fault. I was shattered and filled with shame. My will, desire, and stamina to keep going in the industry was gone. I felt crushed, drained of hope. In this state of devastation, I packed some clothes and, a few days later, got behind the steering wheel of my 2007 BMW and drove 190 miles back home to San Luis Obispo, tears blurring the road for most of the three-hour journey.

By the time I arrived at my folks' place, I had convinced myself that working in my family's Italian restaurant, *Vieni Vai Trattoria* (which aptly translates as "Come and Go" Trattoria), was really what I needed to be doing. Why had I been fighting it all these years? You know, that restaurant was special to me. After school every day, I'd head there to hang out with my dad, and he'd whip up something delicious for me to eat. It's where I had high school dance dinners with my friends. It's where I grew up, surrounded by family working together to make the business thrive. I had always viewed it as a safety net, a plan B, in case my other ventures didn't pan out. While my parents never forced their business onto me, there was an unspoken expectation for me to take the reins eventually. After facing disappointment after disappointment in my pursuit of success in the film industry, I realized it was time to explore my backup plan.

Our restaurant sat in the center of the main drag and attracted a steady stream of locals and tourists. The food was amazing—many of our dishes came from old family recipes. The place had a lively and fun family vibe. My dad was the king of the show, effusively welcoming folks and ushering them to a table inside, a seat out on the patio, or a stool by the green marble wraparound bar he had built with his own hands. The walls had colorful murals of Naples, where many Silvestres still live. It was a welcoming place.

I grew up in the embrace of this sprawling restaurant, and good memories were fixed in my mind. As young as seven years old, I had the job of putting bread on the tables, and by fifteen, I had my own waitressing section. Though I didn't always love the shifts, now as an adult, fresh from the horrors of Hollywood, I felt ready to fall into the open arms of the family business again.

This was just what my parents had wanted all along.

The Silvestres are a fiery bunch. We love fiercely, we work hard, and we fight to the end. My mom is American Irish and grew up in California, while my father, Giuseppe Silvestre was from a small town in the south of Italy. He passed away in March 2023 of esophageal cancer, and he was the hardest-working, boots-on-the-ground guy I've ever known. Like many immigrants, he came to this country with practically nothing except willpower and determination, characteristics he boldly embodied.

My dad was all of five-foot-four, but within that compact frame was enough drama to play every role in all five acts of

Hamlet. For the average American, his histrionics might have seemed over-the-top. For example, he waved his hands to "welcome" customers and crooned like a tenor over a newly imported cheese. There was nothing subtle about my dad.

My mom, on the other hand, generally kept her cool, letting frustration quietly simmer until it boiled over. When she'd had enough of the restaurant's chaos, a plate of lasagna might go flying across the kitchen, turning the staff into silent, sauce-splattered mummies. That, my friends, was life in the family restaurant.

If you are familiar with how things tend to go with family businesses, you know there is often tremendous pressure on the eldest child to take over and continue the legacy regardless of whether they have any genuine interest or passion for it. When my life came crashing down, I took the bait, thinking happiness might lie there. Maybe my parents did know best?

But my dad, like me, had a very strong personality, and we constantly butted heads. He wanted me to do things "his way," while I wanted to find "my way." Whether it was how we presented the menu, what we served, or the way we seated guests, our opinions were on a collision course worthy of the Gran Premio d'Italia. There are lots of moving parts between wait and kitchen staffs, purchasing inventory, promotion, and customer satisfaction, to name a few, and everyone needs to be in sync. The days were fraught with frustration and conflict, a recipe for disaster in the restaurant business.

I had to cover for absentee staff, battle with vendors who overcharged, calm my hot-headed dad, and sometimes put chairs up at the end of the day. At the same time, my friends back in the entertainment industry were getting promoted. While I got calls from former colleagues in LA telling me about their encounters with celebrities and moguls, I was making sure all the tables had a full bottle of olive oil.

My twenties had been a series of "I should be doing" instead of "I would love to be doing," and it turned out that I was repeating the pattern. The restaurant was a beloved family business, but it was not helping me to find my way. No matter how much envy bubbled up while my friends described their lives, I still didn't know what I really wanted to do with my life. Except this: After nearly two years of giving my all to the family business, I was sure I wanted out. My dad was heartbroken, but to his credit, he didn't try to change my mind. He wanted me to be happy.

Why couldn't I be? Was there something wrong with me?

I was now twenty-nine years old and still floundering. The restaurant turned out to be another emotional flop. I had no other options, or so I thought, except to move back to LA, where I returned—without a career, without purpose, single, living off my one credit card, doing odd jobs, and feeling depressed. There were long days when I did nothing more than lie in a fetal position on the kitchen floor, the supposed heart center of the house.

What follows may be triggering or difficult to read—since my depression took a turn into a dark night of the soul—but I want to be forthcoming about my journey and share the truth of what I was feeling. I'll preface it by saying that if you or someone you know needs support, like I did, you can call or text 988 or chat with a support person at 988lifeline.org in the United States. LifeLine is also available worldwide at lifeline-international.com. It doesn't have to be a solo journey.

While time dragged on like a slug for me in LA, I entertained elaborate suicidal thoughts. I didn't fully realize I was stuck in such a deep depression; I was simply lost in its grip. My mind seemed stuck on a negative channel, unable to change the station. The overwhelming feelings of worthlessness and dissatisfaction consumed me, making me question the purpose of continuing on with life in this state. The thought of ending my life loomed ominously if I didn't find a way to combat the constant negativity within me. I imagined fatal accidents, maybe walking across the LA Thruway, swallowing a poisonous concoction, or going into a warm bath and slitting my wrists. I suppose I could have turned to numbing drugs or alcohol as an escape, but I already had enough shame pulsing through my veins that I couldn't consider that route. The never-ending wheel of negative, damning thoughts kept me paralyzed. *I hadn't done enough, wasn't good enough, would always be alone, and would never amount to anything.*

Fortunately, I had always been disciplined, and I made the conscious decision to utilize this trait for positive change. I embarked on a path of self-improvement, seeking solace in neurotherapy, yoga, and meditation groups and devouring every self-help book I could find. I immersed myself in countless mindfulness interviews on YouTube in a desperate bid to turn my life around. It was a pivotal moment when I knew I had to take action in order to survive. Some talk about guardian angels watching over us or a force bigger than we are or a light that guides us. Back then, I couldn't attest to any of this. But my first awareness of a supportive, gentle hand of help occurred when, out of the blue, the fog of misery and hopelessness lifted just enough for me to hear a loving inner voice whisper: *Accept where you are.*

This one sentence cracked me open like a window, and a sliver of light came through. Without thinking, I raised my arms above my head, stretched my body, and felt a shimmer of energy travel up my spine.

That voice released my doomsayer long enough for me to feel some hope.

Okay, so you've made mistakes, the fair inner voice told me. *But you're not a complete failure as a human being.*

This compassionate understanding didn't last forever, but it gave me a break from the negative thought loop that had kept me lying on the floor—and it built me up with enough emotional and physical energy to make it to Sundance. That was where I had my big in-your-face, knock-your-socks-off, shake-rattle-and-roll revelation a few weeks later.

My soul was calling to me. It was time to love myself—*really* love myself—as if it were a full-time job.

Reflecting on my experiences back then, I now realize the importance of honoring every moment in my life. It may not have seemed like it at the time, but everything that happened was essential in shaping my life today. When we're in our twenties, many of us underestimate the value of time. We're itchy and impatient to reach our goals—and then we blame ourselves if we haven't figured everything out within a handful of years. Confused Girl, be patient. You'll get there; everything will fall into place in its perfect moment.

THE TURN AROUND

When negative emotions surface, our first instinct is to bury them. No one loves feeling bad. Yet the only way to return to a positive outlook is to accept all our emotions without judgment.

If we continue to bulldoze through life and bury these negative feelings, eventually we end up smack against that brick wall—or on the floor—crying out in agony.

No need to get to that paralyzing place.

If you don't excavate your feelings, you'll end up prolonging your suffering. Self-loathing grows in silence. If you can accept and allow yourself to feel everything, you'll begin to understand why these emotions live inside you. They're speaking to you.

In my quest to impress those around me, I ended up neglecting my own needs and feelings, completely losing touch with who I really was. I was living for everyone else, and it took a toll on my mental health, plunging me into a deep state of confusion and sadness. It was a real eye-opener to see that chasing external validation wasn't the way to go because it left me feeling lost and disconnected from myself.

Amid all the chaos and unhappiness, I had this moment of clarity when I realized I had to face all these negative emotions head-on to understand that this kind of life just wasn't cutting it for me. I had to own up to my role in creating this mess and start the journey of rediscovering who I truly was and what I wanted out of life. Living by the belief that other people's opinions mattered more than my own had landed me in this rough spot, and I knew deep down that I couldn't keep living like that. It was time to accept where I was at and start figuring things out from there.

On top of that, I also came to the hard truth that I had never felt truly seen, heard, or appreciated throughout my life. How can you be seen, heard, or appreciated when you've been hiding yourself and don't even know who you are? The toxic environments of my past jobs only made those feelings of invisibility worse, leaving me with some emotional scars to work through.

By taking that first step and embracing my unhappiness, I ultimately opened myself up to a new career and life path. I turned toward living in alignment with my authentic self. The same compassionate acceptance is available to you in your current circumstances.

Of course, it would be great if life went exactly as we planned without any disruptions or setbacks, but as Allen Saunders said, "Life is what happens to us while we are busy making other plans."[4] Also, if life was easy, what would be the point of being here?

I've learned so much through my setbacks that I now consider them my greatest gifts. They've propelled me to go further and deeper in my life. These setbacks, coupled with the confusion that comes with them, have empowered me to find my true meaning and purpose in life. Acceptance is finding the power within the pain.

Our experiences are meant to be unpredictable, and many situations are out of our control. By accepting this truth, we can shift our focus from what we cannot change to what we can change. How do we turn those lemons into a pitcher of refreshing, thirst-quenching lemonade? Accept the ingredients you have. Without the confusion, depression, and despair that I found myself in years ago, I would never have written this book.

During this period of unhappiness, I began to dig deep into the weeds and explore the roots of my existence. I asked myself these simple but earth-shattering questions:

Who am I?

How do I really feel? Instead of, *How do I think I should feel?*

Why do I feel this way?

How do I want to feel?

How do I get the feeling that I want?

How do I want to live this life?

These queries are significant. Every one of us has to go through this kind of personal work to find our way. The journey of finding love within ourselves and for ourselves is not just a cliché. It's the fundamental key to living a meaningful life—and it starts with getting curious about who we are and what we're feeling and why, and being compassionate with ourselves. It involves the process of truly seeing our current situation, confronting our fears, and finding our own truth.

I give you my word that there is a purpose to our confusion. When we are courageous enough to embrace it, great things await us. Remember, acceptance doesn't mean complacency. It's a tool that allows us to find peace amid the chaos. It's the process of taking back power.

Acceptance leads to self-compassion, and self-compassion helps us find meaning in even the most difficult experiences. By remaining nonjudgmental, you'll be able to navigate life's challenges with flexibility and resilience, strength and equanimity.

So, love your Confused Girl within. She's your guide. She'll uncover your true, beautiful self and help you find the true purpose in your life.

CONFUSED GIRL RECAP:

- Once upon a time, I embarked on a journey that promised a top-notch education and a ticket to the glitzy world of the film industry. Little did I know this path to success would leave me feeling as sad as a puppy left on the side of the road. Why? Because I was young and lost, living according to what I thought I should be doing, trying to meet the expectations of family, peers, and society.

- I suffered with a severe case of "I'm not good enough." I doubted my abilities and was convinced that any achievement I managed was meager compared to the accomplishments of the folks around me. Comparison is a self-esteem killer.

- My tyrannical mind became a twisted tape loop where self-perceived failures played on repeat. It was as if my brain had its own Netflix channel, streaming a never-ending series of shortcomings.

- I had the blessing of two memorable awakenings. They helped me see that I needed to accept my confusion and embrace it with open arms. It was time to stop pretending and start being real so I could discover the depths of my soul.

- We all travel bumpy roads in our twenties, but every decade of life has something we must discover. Awakenings have their own divine timing, so don't beat yourself up.

- So, my sister Confused Girl, the moral of this chapter is: Don't let a terrific education, the expectations of others, the allure of a glamorous industry, or any dream you think is the be-all and end-all blind you. Accept your emotions, your confusion, your mistakes, and your successes—this acceptance will put you on the path to discovering your true self.

CHAPTER 2

Goodbye, Shame and Guilt

Work on psychological blocks like shame and
guilt—they falsely color your reality.
                                        —Deepak Chopra

After plenty of exhilarating and excruciating ups and downs,
the year 2015 marked a turning point for me as I ventured into
the world of vlogging with the creation of *Confused Girl in the
City*. Every week on YouTube, I poured my thoughts into ep-
isodes, delving into my confusion, sharing what new thing I
was trying that week, and documenting the lessons I was learning. It was my own form of therapy, a cathartic release amid
the chaos of life.

At this time, I also found myself in love with my yoga
practice. On my mat, I could let go and free myself of any obsessive thinking. Never would I have guessed that I would find

inspiration in healing crystals and create a line of yoga wear inspired by these precious stones. But that is exactly what I did! This was during a surge in athleisurewear popularity, but prior to the mainstream adoption of yoga attire. At this time, Lululemon existed as a niche brand known exclusively to passionate yogis.

The full story of how this transformative journey unfolded is a tale best saved for later in the book. However, at this moment, I'll just say that, driven by a desire to follow my heart, I took a leap of faith by launching my line of crystal-inspired yoga wear. I was simultaneously in the process of healing old wounds and embracing a new chapter. So many paths converged that year following my Sundance awakening, and I was saying yes to every door that opened—whether it was an internal or external opportunity to expand.

As I was unraveling the intricacies of my past and the patterns that seemed to repeat in my life, I couldn't help but feel overwhelmed by the lessons I needed to learn and the emotions I needed to face. One of these lessons came through my experiences with the Nordstrom department store. After several months of selling online, I reached out to dozens of department stores, including Nordstrom, a hugely respected fashion retailer that's been around since 1901. I was over the moon when a representative from the company called me back and, with an abundance of enthusiasm, told me that she was going to present my clothing line to the head buyer. "I love, love, love your activewear! I'm obsessed!" she practically exploded. "We'll be in touch!"

When we hung up, my mind floated like a balloon. I imagined my apparel displayed center stage in the department store. I saw Nordstrom placing a full-page ad in a glossy magazine. I even envisioned Oprah (a fan of that department store) choosing my activewear as one of her "favorite things." *What a dream come true!*

Well, the universe had a different plan. The head of purchasing labeled my leggings as "ugly" and "unsuitable for Nordstrom." Obviously, there was no order. A wave of shame rushed in, and I replayed the roaring ocean of rejection. How could I have gotten so swept away in delusion? Hadn't I learned anything? That negative voice in my head grew louder, taunting me with thoughts of inadequacy. *You're kidding yourself to think you have a chance. Your stuff is ugly. You're not cut out for this. You're a poser, a fake, a loser.* Yes, I succumbed to that dark place and allowed those shameful thoughts to pull me under again—though not for long.

I had done enough work on myself over the previous year to be able to examine the truth of the naysayer's words. I reflected on the situation and asked myself: Could it be this Nordstrom buyer was just having a bad day? It seemed plausible. Alternately, maybe she really did see my apparel as ugly. But rather than stay in that pit of despair, I reminded myself that thousands of other women had purchased and proudly worn my clothing; they even boasted about it on social media.

I moved on. This was only one person's opinion, after all, I told myself. I made a conscious decision not to dwell on her negative judgment. Rather, I offered myself a compassionate view. I focused on the overwhelming support and love my products received from so many others. I vowed to forge ahead. I kindly renewed my commitment to be undeterred by folks who don't believe in me. I put the power back in my own hands.

As most of you know, shame and guilt can be devastating.

When these emotions are left unrecognized or untamed, they make our lives tough to navigate and prevent us from reaching our higher selves—that all-knowing, all-powerful, all-loving aspect of us. But don't worry, my fellow Confused Girl! I've discovered how to overcome these negative emotions, and I bear witness to the fact that you, too, can recover your confidence, positivity, and power.

Dealing with shame and guilt, I've learned, is a process, and like most things in life, it takes practice. I'll start by unpacking what shame is, then move on to guilt. This way, we can get a handle on the nuances of each emotion. I'll also get into the steps that have helped me work through these two self-defeating emotions.

SHAME

Shame is about our whole being. It's a feeling of humiliation rooted in a belief that we are inherently unworthy. I now see what a hoax it is, but at one time, shame was an emotion that was all too familiar to me. Instead of acknowledging and processing shame, we tend to internalize it, and it ends up living within us as our dirty little secret. We decide that there's something at our very core that's defective. Does this sound familiar?

Shame comes from being told, probably since childhood— by our parents, by society, by trauma—that we're not enough, that we need to be different from how we are, and that it's not okay to not be okay. This programming, this "wrongness," teaches us to see ourselves, often at a very young age, as defective.

I observed this firsthand several years ago when I was

visiting my friend Nicole in her Venice Beach bungalow. Her infant, Lucas, was making his debut among a half-dozen adoring family members and friends. It was late afternoon, and the light was dimming—a time when many babies get irritable. Little five-week-old Lucas, snug in his onesie, was no exception. He began to fidget . . . and before long was wailing.

Everyone in the room, including me, wanted nothing more than to help Lucas relax and feel better. We immediately flew into action, gathered around this little being, and began making ridiculous gestures, clucking noises, funny faces. Someone broke into a Motown version of "The Itsy Bitsy Spider."

If only our group had been in touch with the author Charles Dickens's advice from his novel *Great Expectations*: "We need never be ashamed of our tears."[5] In our present culture, most parents feel responsible for their offspring's emotional state. I'm not a parent, but I know that my folks felt a hefty amount of discomfort and guilt when they witnessed my emotional upheaval. In turn, seeing their reaction perpetuated a cycle in which my despair doubled. I then reacted by feeling ashamed for contributing to *their* unhappiness. This dynamic put me in a position of rejecting what I was experiencing, ultimately leading to more shame and disconnecting me from how I was truly feeling.

Parents may also experience anger when their kid is hurting because they don't know how to deal with their own ill-placed shame that hasn't been examined and processed. This can result in a blaming reaction. "Why should you be unhappy? We've given you so much. How can you be so ungrateful?" Once again, this can create a negative emotional pattern for the child.

I'm not blaming parents for their responses. I believe we all do the best we can with the awareness we have. Also, I'm not saying we should leave babies in discomfort. I'm just offering an example of how we're taught, even as infants, that it's not okay to not be okay. So, what can we do about it? How can we unlearn this conditioning?

STEP ONE: SELF-REFLECTION

The first step, when dealing with our shame, is self-reflection. We need to take a hard look at what's triggering it. We need to examine those sneaky thoughts and beliefs that fuel this emotion. Then we must acknowledge it. In my experience, a big part of letting go of my shame was telling the truth and letting the world know: *I'm confused.*

I had a realization that not having all the answers, feeling uncertain about my life, and not knowing who I was triggered a deep sense of shame within me. To identify your triggers, it's helpful to observe recurring emotional patterns or reactions. For instance, when I was unemployed and lost, being asked, "What do you do?" would instantly trigger anxiety. It would manifest in my body language and tone of voice. I found myself over-compensating by adopting a serious demeanor, standing taller, and recounting my past achievements as if in a job interview. The discomfort in people's reactions made me acutely aware that they knew they'd touched on a sensitive topic, leaving me feeling embarrassed and ashamed.

Once we recognize these emotional patterns, we can explore the underlying causes of these reactions. This exploration offers an opportunity to reflect on past experiences, childhood memories, or significant life events that may be linked to our triggers. It's essential to remember that when triggered, we often attribute blame to others or the situation itself. At times, someone's words have stirred feelings of sadness and anger in me, and I wished I could make them disappear with a snap of my fingers. However, the pivotal "aha" moment comes with the realization that these emotions stem from within us. No one can make you feel a certain way—our responses are entirely our own.

This is the reason I named my blog and activewear line "Confused Girl in the City." I wanted to bring my so-called shame into the light—and not just for myself but for all women. I know from experience that when a dirty little secret is kept in the dark and left unexamined, it festers and grows, and its villainous roots spread to different areas of our lives.

The remedy? Uncover your shame and release that feeling into the light of authenticity. Accept your feelings as real and slay your Shame Monster.

Be on the lookout. Shame comes in all forms—from body shame to social shame—to whatever BS we believe. Our culture is a cruel mistress. She commands: "Believe *this*." "Look like *this*." "Buy *this*." "Do *this*." "Say *this*—and for God's sake, don't say *that*!" "And if you can't deal with your shame, we have a pill that washes it away." Question the ridiculous rules, and standards society snaps at us like a wet towel. Who says we have to be perfect? How boring would life be if we were perfect? Or if we knew it all? There would be no sense of wonder or discovery.

STEP TWO: SELF-COMPASSION

Eventually, we all encounter individuals who test our self-doubt. Some may be eager to see if we'll crumble under their pressing thumb of judgment. To that, I say, *Thank you for showing me that I have the power to overcome.* And that goes for you, Ms. Nordstrom! Do not allow the haters to shame you. You have innate resilience. Give yourself some love. Self-reflection has this magical way of leading us to a place of self-compassion. When we take the time to understand ourselves, to trace the path we've been on, acknowledging the times we felt defeated and recognizing how we've navigated life, a sense of self-love is sparked. Compassion blooms beautifully from the seeds of reflection and observation.

One thing that helped me during those tough, self-doubting days was my praise folder. I started collecting messages from customers who raved about my leggings and brand, storing them in a special folder. I'd suggest creating your own praise folder or praise journal where you jot down kind words or compliments you receive. It's like a warm hug for your soul on those low-vibe days.

I'm excited to share more about self-love in an upcoming chapter. It's such a rich topic that deserves its own space, so stay tuned for that!

Here's the thing: You deserve to embark on an adventure of a lifetime. *Carry on!* And while you're offering yourself compassion, throw some in the hater's direction too. They can use it.

STEP THREE: SHIFT YOUR MINDSET

How many of us believe we shouldn't have problems or we can't make mistakes? I use the word *mistakes* intentionally in place of the word *failure*. Failure is a cognitive invention and a shame-based bully. It's nothing more than a perspective, and perspectives can be turned around with a little mental magic. Failure isn't a fixed truth; it's more like a belief that can change depending on how you see things. For example, let's say you host a book reading, and only five people show up. Some might look at that and think, *Well, that's a failure*, focusing on the small turnout. But then, there's another way to see it. Someone else could see those five attendees and think, *Hey, this is pretty cool!* They might appreciate the intimate vibe, the chance for deeper connections, and the quality time with each person there.

This scenario shows how success and failure aren't set in stone. It all comes down to how you view things, what you value, and what you consider important. By understanding that failure is subjective and open to interpretation, you can start seeing setbacks in a new light. It's all about shifting your perspective and understanding that every experience, no matter how it turns out, can teach you something valuable and offer you a way to move forward.

Failure keeps us stagnant and oppressed by our anxiety. Fear of failure blocks our creativity. It holds us back from taking action, from trying something new. After working hard on myself and understanding the path to personal freedom, I can no longer compute the concept of failure.

Another thing I've learned is that timing is important. You don't want to make premature moves because you're looking for the first exit out of shame. When life throws us a mind-boggling predicament, the best move forward may be to simply observe and reflect until we understand what's going on. To the outside world, it may look like we're not doing anything, but through self-observation we can learn invaluable lessons. As Ecclesiastes says, "For everything there is a season, and a time for every matter under heaven."[6]

When it's time to take action, life demands that we try, even if it means dancing with the unknown. If you don't take the opportunity, you're telling the universe you don't want the gift.

Question whether it's still your shame saying, *I don't deserve it* or *I'm afraid I'll fail.* We must step outside our comfort zones and take these opportunities to live a full life.

We all face challenges, and some bring us to our knees. But if we rise up, we become the heroes of our own story. We emerge with a stronger sense of self-worth. Take a moment to reflect on someone you deeply admire. Isn't one of the reasons they hold a special place in your heart because they conquered adversity? I'll give you a few of my favorites: J. K. Rowling, Rosa Parks, and Malala Yousafzai. There are plenty more; maybe your example of resilience was set by your grandmother, aunt, teacher, or friend.

In case I haven't convinced you yet, let me share another story that illustrates how putting all three steps in place can help you heal from shame and rise higher. When I was in my late twenties, having just returned to LA from the restaurant—depressed, hating my life, and lying on the floor of my apartment in tears—I found myself attending a meditation group that called itself "Against the Stream." Every Wednesday, around twenty-five men and women between the ages of twenty and forty gathered in a nondescript brick building in Santa Monica. Most were recovering from drug and alcohol addiction, while I was there trying to recover from my addiction to negative thinking.

We sat in a circle on gray metal folding chairs, our feet planted on the wood floor, eyes cast on our laps to avoid the cruel fluorescent lighting. After the leader of the group rang a bell, we sat in silence for forty-five minutes. At the end of the meditation, the leader would ask, "What came up for you?"

Several gatherings passed before I was willing or capable of sharing, but one evening, I had no choice. Only a couple of days earlier, another boyfriend, a man I had believed would be my companion forever, had broken up with me. I had had a string of going-nowhere relationships, but this one was a shock that left me fractured. I felt unlovable. I felt unworthy. I felt ugly. I felt undesirable. I was my own worst-case scenario.

I somehow dragged myself to meditation and sat my sorry butt on the metal chair, sobbing through the forty-five minutes of attempted silence. When it was over and time to share, I used Step One: Self-Reflection and allowed my heart to speak out loud, unfiltered—I was able to hear myself. Everyone in the circle seemed to understand. I wasn't alone. Many had been through similar experiences, they told me. I was vulnerable, but I was being held safely within their compassion. One person after another reminded me that I was not a failure. There was no reason to feel shame. I was worthy. I want to note that it wasn't about the external validation but more about allowing myself to be vulnerable and reflect on how I was feeling. Hearing that I wasn't alone was a beautiful outcome of this moment.

In the safety of the meditation group, I was heard, and because of this, I was willing to accept their words of assurance with Step Two: Self-Compassion. Okay, I hurt. I had good reason to feel hurt. But there was no reason to wrap shame around it. I would heal. For now, I needed to cry my heart out—and I gave myself permission to do it. I acknowledged my pain and validated my feelings without layering shame upon them. I recognized the validity of my hurt and released it through tears, allowing the healing process to begin. Through the lens of others' empathy, I gained a fresh perspective that had eluded me in my internal dialogue. Their compassion became a mirror to reflect self-compassion. At times, it takes witnessing compassion in action to learn how to extend it to yourself.

Looking back, I'm grateful for those Wednesday gatherings. The group was a safe place where I could confront and challenge the negative beliefs that had taken up residency in my head. In good part thanks to my meditating comrades, I now stand as a testament to the power of self-love. You don't have to be alone in this shame-fighting battle. Rally the troops! Maybe a trusted friend, family member, therapist, or support group can be there for you. Sharing our experiences and vulnerabilities is a game changer. Removing your emotional armor takes bravery and tenacity, but it will only make you a more powerful warrior.

With this practice, I learned that by exploring and expressing my hurt without shame, I would gain access to my compassionate soul. Eager to shift my mindset, I was ready for Step Three. From the vantage point of self-compassion, my mind naturally shifted from seeing the world as a place of judgment to a place of love. Though I may have stumbled through it the first time around, returning to these steps time and time again helped me use my breakup as a catalyst for change. This shift in perspective allowed me to understand that I never truly fail; I simply learn and grow from every experience, becoming stronger and more resilient. Failure doesn't exist in my vocabulary anymore; it's just a stepping stone toward personal development. This realization has transformed me into a person who approaches challenges with a mindset of self-compassion.

GUILT

Now that we've kicked shame to the curb, let's dig into guilt. *Guilt* is a feeling of remorse or regret for something we did or did not do. It can also be a feeling of deep worry or unhappiness that we've done something wrong, causing harm to another person—a perceived burden of responsibility for someone else.

Whether it's a cringe-worthy mistake, a hurtful action, a golden opportunity we let slip by, or religious guilt because we're not pious enough, if we don't deal with the heavy weight of guilt, it can drag us down. But fear not, Confused Girl! Once we empower ourselves with those three kickass steps, we can embark on an adventure of self-forgiveness. We can also give guilt the boot.

Keep in mind that guilt isn't an emotion we necessarily create on our own. It is a complex emotion that can be influenced by external factors as well as our own thoughts and actions. Religious guilt is a good example. Personally, I got my dose of indoctrinated guilt growing up in a Catholic family—starting with the guilt of original sin and then going on from there. Endless. Research shows that Catholics and Protestants experience "higher levels of maladaptive interpersonal guilt than those with no religious affiliation."[7] Even the rich and famous are susceptible to Catholic guilt. Actor Bradley Cooper copped to it: "Unfortunately, when someone asks me for a favor, I can't say no. Because of my upbringing—my Catholic guilt—if I don't do it, it plagues me."[8]

I get it, Bradley, but thank God, I rarely feel the emotion of guilt anymore. On those rare instances when I do, I ask myself, "Is this *my* guilt? Or does this originate from years of being conditioned to feel this way?"

Let's reflect on a recent instance when you felt guilty about something. Ask yourself: *Why did I feel guilty about this? Is it because I made a serious mistake, or is it from feeling like I should have done something (aka conditioning)?* Or maybe it's a bit of both. If you find that it's because of conditioning, it's crucial to question your perspective—what do *you* really feel and believe? And how does or doesn't that change how you handled it?

I carried a lot of guilt for having sex before marriage. I went to Catholic schools my entire life, and the nuns and other educators laid a heavy guilt trip on us. The Catholic church's doctrine forbids fornication, calling it a "mortal sin" and describing it as "gravely contrary to the dignity of persons and of human sexuality."[9] You get the picture.

I hold deep appreciation for my Catholic upbringing. It instilled many valuable principles that have guided me well in life. It taught me the importance of ironing my T-shirts so that I present myself neatly to the world. And it taught me to always be on time. The Sisters were so insistent on punctuality; just a minute late and you were in dreaded after-school detention. I'm making light of the church's teachings, but I want to be clear that I have the utmost respect for all religions and firmly believe that their core teachings are rooted in love. It's just the inherent nature of humans, with our blend of positive and negative perspectives, that often leads religion into the chaotic landscape of hypocrisy. That's duality for you.

In my late twenties, the guilt surrounding premarital sex resurfaced, even though I was now a fully independent woman. I was financially independent, lived on my own, traveled extensively, and had an impressive résumé. But one weekend I was back in my hometown and instantly morphed into a guilty adolescent again. I felt compelled to lie to my folks and say that I wouldn't be staying with them because I was sleeping at my friend Anna's house. In truth, I was sleeping with an old boyfriend.

My mom must have suspected something because she phoned Anna's parents' house and found out I wasn't there. When I got back to the family home the next morning after a steamy night of great sex, my mom combusted. She threw my first communion picture on the floor and shot a sizzling death-ray stare straight into my eyes. "I never brought you up to behave like this!" she blasted.

After this incident, I made a conscious decision that my Catholic guilt no longer aligned with my personal beliefs. *Basta!* It was, and still is, perfectly acceptable if others hold a different view, but I had to release my burden of guilt; it was weighing me down and I was acting contrary to my beliefs. I knew I hadn't done anything "wrong," and I reminded myself of that until it took hold in my soul. This was me having self-compassion for myself. Then I shifted my thinking. I acknowledged that I was now guided by my own moral compass.

But how does one truly let go of rules deeply ingrained in your psyche since childhood?

I found a way, but I admit it's pretty theatrical. Letting go is a matter of individual style—sort of like leggings. My technique was to take an epic walk along the incandescent Santa Monica and Venice Beaches at sunrise. I wasn't just strolling aimlessly. I was on a mission to rid myself of the weighty burden of guilt. I imagined that I was carrying a heavy backpack filled with my past regressions—all the times I had lied or felt guilty about my sexuality. About halfway along the route, I tossed this imaginary backpack into the vastness of the Pacific Ocean, and with the dramatic release of my baggage, I became lighter, taller, and much freer.

If you find this method too over-the-top, no problem. You can concoct your own version to release the weight from your shoulders. Perhaps it's more your style to visualize soaring like a graceful seagull and dropping your guilt from above into the vast sea. Or you might feel more empowered by having a release ceremony. Write your guilty regrets on bits of paper and then set them safely aflame.

It's also worth noting that guilt has the potential to be a positive force in some instances. Guilt can show us that we're not oblivious to how our actions affect others. I like to see guilt as the catalyst that drives us towards introspection and self-awareness. If guilt is raining on your parade, you'll probably feel so uncomfortable you'll be motivated to take steps to remedy the situation. You'll have the desire to work it out, apologize, make amends, or change your behavior. By giving guilt a proper place in our lives, we can use it to be more empathetic, to maintain our integrity, and to develop stronger connections with others. Within reason, it can be our personal character trainer. It pushes us to care about the potential harm we've caused. Through reflecting on our actions and recognizing the impact they have on others, guilt can help us learn from our mistakes and strive to become better people. It's like a little nudge that pushes us to be more understanding and just all-around better humans. So, instead of shying away from guilt, we can use it as a tool for personal growth and moral development.

THE ART OF THE APOLOGY AND THE GIFT OF FORGIVENESS

Part of becoming better humans, especially when it comes to guilt, is learning the art of apology, as well as the ability to forgive.

I am a huge fan of sincere amends. If I've hurt or offended someone, I make it my mission to seek forgiveness. In turn, if someone crushes me, I work on opening my heart and letting the hurt go. I don't mean in a superficial way. I mean deep down.

Here's the thing: The ego hates apologizing, and it's not too keen on forgiving either. The ego is a tough cookie—it always wants to be the hero. It loves feeling superior and struggles with vulnerability and self-reflection. So, when we're stuck in our heads, overthinking and caught up in those ego-driven stories, forgiving and apologizing can feel like climbing Mount Everest. But hey, there's hope! By tuning in to our emotions, practicing mindfulness, and ditching old patterns, we can calm down our egos and open our hearts to forgiveness and understanding. It's all about letting go of the need to be right and being open to a more loving and authentic way of living. Personal growth and transformation are within reach once we put that ego in its place and lead with humility and empathy.

Forgiveness takes time—forgiving yourself or forgiving others. You can begin by self-reflection. Are you struggling to forgive someone? What is making it difficult for you? Ask yourself, what might have brought this person to take such an action? And what was your role? Have you noticed how holding on to grudges affects your mental and emotional well-being? You can also reflect on times when others have forgiven you. Have you experienced how forgiveness can lead to healing and rebuilding relationships in your own life? Forgiveness is a gift that we give ourselves and others. When we choose to forgive, it's like lifting a heavy weight off our shoulders and freeing ourselves from all that negative stuff, like anger and resentment. It allows us to move forward with a sense of peace and clarity and gives us the space to grow. And it's good not just for us—forgiving someone can also be a gift to them. It opens up the possibility of reconnection through trust and understanding, and it can bring people closer together. Forgiveness is an act of kindness and love that has the power to make things better for everyone involved.

When you've caused the offense, offer a graceful apology by acknowledging the misdeed, taking responsibility, and expressing remorse. Then move on to self-compassion and forgive yourself. Forgive yourself for all the things you did or didn't do, for all the words you said or left unsaid. When I need to apologize to myself, I place my hands over my heart and speak these words:

I forgive you.

I love you.

I'm proud of you.

Now release this burden.

You can do this every single day until you feel the weight of guilt and shame lift from your shoulders—and trust me, you will feel it.

Remember, every single person on this planet is dealing with their own feelings of guilt and shame. We're not alone. We're all part of the grand human race. And you know what? All our difficult experiences and overwhelming emotions are beautiful opportunities for transformation.

ACCEPT YOURSELF IN THIS MOMENT

Fact of life: Humans screw up, sometimes big-time. Accepting our humanity and imperfections is one of the guiding principles behind naming my brand "Confused Girl in the City." Some people vibe with it and appreciate its authenticity, while others are offended by the name. When someone puts it down, I suspect it might be because they're carrying their own shame for not having it all figured out. They have yet to understand that *not having it all figured out* is an opportunity.

One woman suggested I rename my company "Grounded Girl." Look, I get it. We all prefer to have our feet planted safely on the ground rather than teeter on the uneven surface of confusion. I was feeling pretty grounded when I was writing from the balcony of my guesthouse in Ubud, Bali, gazing on rice terraces the color of jade and breathing in the sweet scent of incense and flowers wafting through the air. Every morning the host mother of the guesthouse placed a thin stick of incense surrounded by colorful flower petals on our doorsteps in reverence for the gods. It was a ritualistic offering. This daily gesture became my own morning ritual on the island, a moment of gratitude for the beauty and spirituality surrounding me.

But this emotional and environmental paradise doesn't last forever. Inevitably, I'll always find myself bewildered by a new twist, in a new place, with new things being asked of me. That's life. When it happens, I'll be ready to uncover something beautiful and fresh about myself. Being a grounded girl doesn't require the same support as a confused girl. It's easy-peasy to accept yourself when everything is going swell and your life is on track. But it's not so simple when things get sticky and uncertain. We tend to shame ourselves precisely when we desperately need to give ourselves loving support.

"Confused Girl" is about allowing yourself to be vulnerable and accepting where you are, just as you are, in this very moment. I firmly believe self-reflection, compassion for yourself and others, and a shift in how you see your predicament will guide you out of the landscape of shame and guilt. In its place is . . . illumination.

Now can you see the path ahead?

CONFUSED GIRL RECAP:

- It's time to dive deep into the world of self-reflection! Buckle up because you're about to embark on a shame-busting journey that will leave you feeling empowered and ready to conquer the world. The first step in overcoming shame is to take a good, hard look at the triggers that set it off. I'm talking about those sneaky beliefs and thoughts that fuel our shame and make us feel like we're carrying the weight of the world on our shoulders. To identify your triggers, it's helpful to observe recurring emotional patterns or reactions. Once we recognize these emotional patterns, we can explore the underlying causes of these reactions. It's time to grab a magnifying glass and examine them like a detective.

- Instead of wallowing in self-pity, let's activate our inner female warrior and embrace vulnerability. Yes, you heard me right. We're going to be unafraid and open up to others about our shame and guilt. It's time to bring those buried feelings to the light so they can lose their power over us. After all, what lurks in the dark controls us, and we're not about that life anymore.

- Guilt can really drag us down, right? It's like this heavy weight that stops us from growing. But once we dig into where that guilt comes from—whether it's from religious teachings or societal pressures—and show ourselves some self-love, we can start letting go of that burden and live in line with what truly matters to us. And you know what? Guilt can be good if we use it to learn more about ourselves, show empathy, and grow in understanding.

- Now, here's where things get fabulously theatrical. Try my funny backpack ritual. Picture this: You grab a backpack, fill it with all your shame and insecurities, and then dramatically throw it to the wind. Imagine the wind catching it and carrying it away, leaving you feeling lighter and freer than ever before. It's a symbolic gesture that says, "Hey, shame and guilt, I'm done with you. Bye-bye!"

- But hold on tight because we're not done yet. This next step is crucial. We need to be kind to ourselves. And I mean really kind. No more beating ourselves up for past blunders. We're all human, and guess what? Humans screw up sometimes. It's part of our charm, really. Whether it's something you did to someone else or even yourself, it's time to make it your mission to seek forgiveness. Pick up that phone, dial the number, and ask for forgiveness. It may feel uncomfortable, but trust me, the weight that will be lifted off your shoulders will be worth it. And don't forget the most important part: forgive yourself. Look at yourself in the mirror, give yourself a wink, and say, "Hey, I messed up, but I'm ready to move on and be a better version of myself." You've got this!

CHAPTER 3

Mirror, Mirror

There is no one alive who is you-er than you.

—Dr. Seuss

One night I was weaving my way through the lively crowds in Chiang Mai's bustling marketplace. There, the markets are woven seamlessly through the city's ornate temples. The air was alive with the sounds of vendors hawking their goods, the chatter of locals and tourists blending together in a symphony of languages. I loved the vibrant colors of the market stalls, the smells of street food sizzling on grills, the pungent tang of herbs and spices piled high in colorful displays, the sweet scent of tropical fruits, and even the unpleasant sewage stench lurking beneath it all. You could feel the energy in the air, the excitement of discovering new sights and sounds around every corner. Yet there was also a tranquil side to this city—one I immersed myself in. I couldn't help but compare my time in Thailand to my time back in Bali, where the acres of rice fields and the chatterbox monkeys held me under their spell. The thing is, both have their charms.

There's an eternal debate of Bali versus Thailand, a topic that ignites fiery discussions among us digital nomads—by that, I mean those of us earning our living by working online in various locations of our choosing. In 2017, I was struck with the idea of writing this book, but I knew that staying within my comfort zone wouldn't cut it. I craved adventure, seeking inspiration from the world around me. Traveling and exploring new destinations have always ignited a fire within me, bringing my soul to life. I yearned to immerse myself in settings that would fuel my creativity and make me feel truly alive. Making a pledge to myself, I set out to write this book while living abroad.

It took me a year to transform my activewear business into a fully mobile operation, allowing me the freedom to work from anywhere. Finally, in 2018, I was ready to embark on this new chapter of my life. With just one suitcase, a backpack, and my trusty laptop in tow, I set off on my quest toward peace, inspiration, and the fulfillment of a long-held dream.

While I was living in Bali for several life-changing months, I discovered that many digital nomads flock to Chiang Mai, especially during Bali's rainy season, November to April. I got the tip from fellow expats at a coworking event in Ubud. I decided to take their advice and head to Chiang Mai in December. One evening, while hanging out with other expats at an entrepreneur event in a Chiang Mai hotel, we sat around the pool debating which paradise was better: Bali's wet season, which I enjoy, versus Chiang Mai's sunny allure. Here's the conundrum: How can we compare two places that are both spectacular, yet as different as night and day? It's like trying to compare a yummy Thai curry to a mouthwatering Balinese Babi Guling (that's a suckling pig feast, btw). Utterly impossible, I tell you!

Sure, we can list the things we prefer, but let's be honest, it all comes down to personal taste. It's a matter of individual connection, not a competition to determine a winner. Also, our connections and preferences change during different parts of our lives. I, for one, have a deep-rooted affection for Bali—the only place where I have felt completely free from anxiety—while the person I was chatting with found more pleasure in Chiang Mai.

Oh, comparisons . . . We can't help ourselves, can we?

Our brains are wired to evaluate not only different products, philosophies, countries, cultures, and foods—but also how we measure up to other people. This practice divides rather than unites us. It dismisses the Hindu belief of "all one" and the Buddhist's concept of "nothingness." The concept of "all one" means that everything in the universe is connected and comes from the same divine source. It's all about unity and how we're all linked together in some way. Buddhism talks about nothingness, which might sound a bit intense, but it's really about letting go of attachments and illusions so you can free yourself from suffering—and find freedom and enlightenment. It's all about feeling connected, finding peace, and letting go of the things that hold us back.

Comparisons can be traced back to ancient human societies. The tendency to compare ourselves to others stems from a natural desire for social connection, status, and a sense of belonging and safety within a community. Over time, comparisons have evolved to play a significant role in shaping human behavior, motivations, decision-making, and social interactions. Many Westerners are conditioned to compete the moment we pop into this world. From the time we're little munchkins, we're told to be the best and shine like stars. Whether it's slaying on the sports field, acing exams, looking like a supermodel, or living in a fancy neighborhood, comparisons lurk at every corner, ready to make us feel inadequate.

I remember my elementary school days as a battleground of competition, where honor roll students were celebrated like superheroes and those who didn't make the list were made to feel invisible. Picture this: The entire school gathered, faculty and parents included, as the principal announced the names of those glorious honor roll achievers. If you made the cut, oh boy, your mom would flaunt a bumper sticker that boasted: *I'm the proud parent of an honor roll student.* But if you didn't make the grade, the pressure and weight of disappointment were excruciating. It sounds hilarious now, but back then, it was a nightmare.

I should know. Having proudly made the honor roll in previous grades, not making the cut in seventh grade came as a significant blow. Sadly, that year, I found myself struggling. Oh, the shame! Oh, the humiliation! As my classmates were individually called up to the stage in the auditorium, I sat there frozen, my mouth as dry as chalk. It wasn't just about me; I also felt like I had let down my family. My father, being a competitive person, had high expectations for me, and the school's emphasis on academic achievement only added to the pressure. It felt like a monumental failure on my part.

That experience not only scarred me, but it also lit a fire. I vowed, *Never again!* Sure, you could say it worked because my grades reached new heights the next semester, but it also taught me that my value was based on achievements—not on other attributes like creativity, kindness, or integrity.

Looking back, I realize that the whole honor roll fiasco was about comparing my self-worth to arbitrary standards. I was caught in a never-ending game of "Who's better?" But here's the thing, my friend: We don't have to play that game. We can define our own self-worth, set our own standards. The world may be a competitive place, where the best grades get you into the best colleges and the highest sales numbers get you that promotion, but we don't have to let those comparisons define us. I can tell you without an iota of doubt that's not who we are.

In her book *Forgiveness*, inspirational speaker Iyanla Vanzant wrote, "Comparison is an act of violence against the self."[10] That's why I'm suggesting a rebellion against the tyranny of comparisons. Let's take back our power, shall we? Let's stop comparing ourselves to others who are not like us, who don't share our unique history, talents, goals, and aspirations. Let's honor our individuality and celebrate our personal path. Because at the end of the day, it's not about being better than anyone else or striving for perfection. It's about being the best version of ourselves, quirks and all.

But hold on. There's some nuance to comparison that I'd like us to break down together. Comparisons don't always hurt our well-being. Yes, they can be a double-edged sword; they can unleash the green-eyed monster of envy and slice through our self-esteem. They also have the power to ignite our motivation, shed light on our strengths, and offer valuable insights. So, let's take a deeper dive into the light and dark sides of the comparison dynamic. When used wisely, comparison can inspire, enlighten, and ignite compassion and gratitude.

HELPFUL COMPARISONS

COMPARISONS CAN BE A SOURCE OF INSPIRATION
AND MOTIVATION.

Have you ever seen someone achieve something amazing and thought, *Hey, if they can do it, so can I?* Witnessing someone else achieve great things can act like a firecracker exploding in our being. Suddenly, we're filled with a burning desire to chase after our own brilliance. Often, the qualities we admire in others are reflections of the strengths we already possess within ourselves that have yet to be used. The flaws we see in others may be aspects of ourselves that we judge and have yet to embrace fully. By comparing ourselves to those we look up to, we are holding up a mirror to our potential and recognizing the traits we already possess but may need to cultivate further.

I remember when I desperately wanted to travel, but I was waiting for a boyfriend to come into my life or a friend or colleague to be available. When you wait for another person to become your travel buddy . . . well, good luck. At the same time, I realized there was a girl I knew who was constantly going off to fabulous destinations and having solo adventures around the world. I couldn't help but be a bit jealous—and also in awe. She would talk on and on about all the fascinating people she met and the wild adventures she had. *I wanted that too!*

I began to compare my ability to travel solo against her ability. We both had about the same income, we were both street savvy, we were both outgoing with a knack for communication, and we were both capable of being solitary souls, enjoying our own company. I came to the conclusion that I was holding back because of fear. What would I do alone on a long trip? Isn't it better to share experiences with someone? Would I be lonely? Would I get homesick? What if I came across a dangerous situation? Could I protect myself? Would I get lost? Oh my gosh, what if my phone was stolen?

Rather than continue subjecting myself to a toxic blend of fear and envy, I made the conscious choice to open up to her about my anxieties. I asked whether she had ever experienced loneliness while traveling and missed having someone to share those moments with. Her response was enlightening: "Loneliness is a part of being human, but most of the time, I'm immersed in the new surroundings. Each trip unfolds in its own unique way, and I adapt and learn along the way. I often find that I connect with more people when traveling solo than when I have a travel companion." Her words of encouragement reassured me of my inner strength and intuition—that I could safeguard myself and navigate any potentially risky situations and emotional lows. My conclusion was that if she could do it, I could as well. And that, my friend, was the start of my independent travels.

So, thank you, comparison, for giving me that inspired kick in the rear!

COMPARISONS CAN PROVIDE US WITH VALUABLE INSIGHTS AND LEARNING OPPORTUNITIES.

Take makeup foundations, for example. You've got one that gives you that flawless, full-coverage look and another that's all about that fresh, natural vibe. By trying them out side by side, you can see which one feels right for your skin and gives you the look you're going for. So, comparing makeup products is like your own personal beauty trial-and-error session that helps you find the perfect foundation to help you feel like the best version of yourself. Makeup is a low-stakes example of how comparing and contrasting can be a secret weapon in our decision-making arsenal. By pitting different ideas, products, or approaches against each other, we can uncover their strengths and weaknesses—and what's right for *us*.

Now, what if you're facing a conflict with your mom, and your usual approach is to get angry and let things escalate into a heated argument? You might compare your knee-jerk reaction to a different approach. What if, instead of reacting with anger, you calmly express your feelings without raising your voice? By comparing these two approaches, you're exploring how each one plays out and considering which might be more effective in resolving the conflict. Maybe you realize that the calm, nonconfrontational approach allows for better communication and understanding, leading to a more constructive resolution. Through this comparison, you're gaining insight into your behavior and potentially discovering a more successful way to address conflicts with your mom.

Armed with more knowledge about ourselves, we become decision-making ninjas, selecting the best option that suits our individual needs and preferences. So, thank you, comparisons, for helping me make informed makeup choices and resolve conflicts with my mom.

COMPARISONS CAN FOSTER A SENSE OF GRATITUDE AND APPRECIATION.

When we're caught up in our day-to-day lives, it's easy to take things for granted and lose sight of the bigger picture. Comparisons can serve as a wake-up call, prompting us to reflect on our own blessings and privileges. By comparing our situation to those less fortunate, we gain a new perspective that fosters appreciation for what we have right in front of us. This shift in mindset not only helps us recognize the abundance in our lives but also encourages us to be more mindful and empathetic toward others. It's a reminder to cherish what we have and to approach life with a sense of humility and gratitude.

Even before I spent time in Bali in 2018, I had decided I wanted to sponsor a child there. I was drawn to an orphanage that was established after the terrorist bombing in Kuta, which took the lives of 202 people. The Balinese organization provided a home and assistance with education and care to kids. I donated 5 percent of my profits from my activewear line to the foundation and some of my customers also donated to the cause, which was particularly heartwarming.

When I arrived in Bali, I finally visited the orphanage and was overwhelmed. The children were cheerful, open, warm, and affectionate. They gathered around me, offering smiles and hugs. But when one of the administrators told me that most of the children had been abused, I lost it. How could anyone abuse or abandon these innocents? It was difficult to hear firsthand about the struggles they had endured. When I compared the circumstances of these children with my experiences growing up, my personal history was put in a new perspective.

If we can open ourselves to the experiences of others, we're given the opportunity to welcome our own blessings. This realization not only releases our hearts into gratitude but also fuels our compassion. It pushes us to contribute positively to society because, hey, we're all in this together. It's not just about us; it's about supporting our global community too.

So, thank you, comparisons, for reminding us to count our blessings and spread some love.

HURTFUL COMPARISONS

COMPARISON CAN TAKE YOU ON A ROLLER-COASTER RIDE OF UNCOMFORTABLE EMOTIONS.

Picture this: You and your friend Poppy both apply to your dream university. Poppy, lucky girl, gets accepted, while you receive a rejection letter. Suddenly, your sense of self-worth sinks as you believe she must be smarter than you. Or let's flip the script. You triumphantly secure a spot at the university, making you feel like a shining star, but poor Poppy is left in the dust. Now, you find yourself strutting around with an air of superiority, not giving much thought to your friend's disappointment. Pull back the curtain and you'll see your sense of superiority is the product of your ego's imagination. That's often the case.

Even when we're feeling great about our performance, unless we've done our work, when the high fades, we can find ourselves back in the same pit of shame and guilt that we examined in the second chapter.

Let's go on another roller-coaster ride. Imagine you and Poppy decide to celebrate your acceptance by hitting the town. As luck would have it, there's a drop-dead gorgeous guy at the bar, catching the attention of both of you. But alas, he only has eyes for Poppy. Ouch! Talk about a blow to the ego. Suddenly, you feel like a wilted flower compared to Poppy's radiant bloom. One moment, you're soaring high, and the next, you're crashing to the ground.

Having an overblown ego can disconnect us from reality

and the people around us. It's like wearing blinders that prevent us from seeing things as they truly are. On the other hand, undervaluing ourselves can also have a similar effect. When we're so occupied with scrutinizing ourselves, picking out every little flaw, and sabotaging our self-confidence, we forget to see our own beauty. A gloomy self-image can put a damper on personal growth and blind us to our dazzling uniqueness. It's important to find that balance, to stay grounded like a tree with strong roots. We can acknowledge our worth, while also staying connected and rooted in the world around us. No thanks, comparison. I'm getting off the roller-coaster ride and following a sure-footed path.

COMPARISONS ARE UNRELIABLE.

In the section on helpful comparison, we talked about how envy can actually be a good thing—it can show us what's possible and give us that extra push to reach our goals. But there's also a darker side to envy. It can bring up feelings of anger and resentment, leading to negative behaviors like gossiping and talking badly about others. It's crucial to keep in mind that what we see is only a small part of the whole story, and comparing ourselves to others based on that limited view can be misleading. Each person's life is unique and complex, so it's not fair to judge ourselves based on the perceived success of someone else. Trust your intuition and remember that no one is above or beneath you—we're all on our own paths.

I keep this truth in mind by remembering a girl I knew in college who seemed to have it all. She was a walking masterpiece, with a body that made heads spin, a swoon-worthy boyfriend, a stunning wardrobe, and a 4.0 GPA. Plus, she was super popular—adoring friends were always swarming around her. I couldn't help but feel a pang of envy as I compared myself to this queen bee.

Whenever I used to reflect on my college days and she popped into my mind, I couldn't help but think to myself, *I bet she has it all—the successful career, the money, the good looks, the gorgeous, doting husband, and two beautiful children, one boy and one girl, of course. Meanwhile, I'm over here confused as hell.* A decade after college, believing the story I'd created of this girl's life, I stumbled upon a heartbreaking post on social media. This seemingly flawless woman had battled cancer in her late twenties and tragically lost her life at the young age of thirty-one. Suddenly, my envy transformed into a deep sense of sorrow for her and her family. At that moment, I couldn't help but feel a tinge of shame for my past jealousy.

No thanks, comparison. I reserve judgment and choose to accept that we all lead complex lives.

THE FIVE GUIDING PRINCIPLES

These five tools I'm about to share have been an absolute game changer for me when it comes to dealing with all the comparisons and pressures society throws our way. I've really honed these principles over time, and they're like my secret weapon in keeping myself on track. Whenever I find myself veering off course, I turn to these principles to realign with my values. Think of them like a trusty compass, leading us toward self-acceptance, meaningful connections, and a life that truly feels satisfying. Are you ready to dive into them?

STAY IN YOUR LANE

It's easy to think we know all about someone else's life. But that's an illusion. We don't know the inner battles they're fighting, the experiences they're having day in and day out, or the traumas they've experienced. We're only comparing ourselves to a projection. How can we avoid making assumptions? I follow the advice my father gave me: "Stay in your lane, Giovanna."

Now, let me tell you, Italians have a knack for packing multiple meanings into their words of wisdom. In this case, the advice means to focus on your own path and explore it to the fullest. Because at the end of the day, that's all we can do. Everything else is simply none of our business. But let me be clear: This doesn't mean you should stay in your comfort zone.

GIVE YOURSELF THE LOVE

In the process of overcoming an impulse to make comparisons, I urge you to *please* be compassionate with yourself. Throughout history, women have been pitted against each other, encouraged to compete for scraps of power. It's time to put an end to that. We all have our insecurities and areas in our lives that we want to improve. For some, it might be personality. I had a friend tell me she was envious of my ability to make people laugh, even though so many folks are drawn to her warmth and intelligence. I have another friend who is constantly comparing her happy marriage to other couples' relationships and feeling as if hers comes up short.

This competitive mindset doesn't just create a little tension; it's a noose that can choke the joy out of us. Jealousy and resentment limit everyone's potential and drain our happiness.

We have to accept that we're not all the same; we have strengths and weaknesses. Some of us are graced with beauty, others with smarts. Some women are natural leaders, others born healers. That, my friends, is what makes the world so interesting. Remember to cherish and appreciate the unique wonders that define who you are, and extend that same appreciation to others. With love for ourselves and love for the extraordinary qualities that others bring, we can live in the richness of humanity and celebrate its vibrant colors.

EMBRACE COLLABORATION

The workplace is where comparisons often take hold in a death grip, creating an atmosphere where colleagues are constantly sizing each other up, ready to pounce at any moment. It's every individual for themselves, with no room for trust or camaraderie. It's a battlefield, but instead of guns and grenades, it's all about who can come up with the snappiest comeback or the most impressive PowerPoint presentation.

I've worked in environments like this, and it's no fun. This is part of the reason I fly solo now. My sensitive self can no longer take these emotionally unhealthy environments.

So, my friend, it's time for radical rebellion and self-love in the face of this toxicity. Let's challenge the status quo and transform these unhealthy environments into spaces of growth and collaboration. By promoting authenticity, active listening, appreciation, collaboration, and a growth mindset, we can create a workplace where trust, support, and team spirit thrive. For example, instead of criticizing a coworker for making a mistake, we could offer constructive feedback and support to help them improve. This slight shift in perspective can lead to a more positive and collaborative work environment, where team members feel valued and supported in their growth and development. Let's lead by example, build connections based on mutual respect, and foster a culture that values individual contributions while championing collective success. Together, we can shift the paradigm from competition to collaboration, creating a more fulfilling work environment for all.

PRACTICE APPRECIATION

Let's appreciate the beauty in our individuality and the talents that make us shine. Because when we stop comparing ourselves to others, we create room for self-love and acceptance. It also allows us to start appreciating the beauty and individuality in others. For those struggling with low self-esteem, recognizing personal strengths may be challenging.

One exercise to cultivate self-appreciation is to sit with a friend and mutually write appreciative notes to each other, highlighting the qualities and strengths that you admire. This exercise can help you see your beauty and unique attributes through the eyes of someone who cares for you. Following this, take some time to write notes of appreciation for yourself, focusing on the qualities that make you special and valued.

To those who find it difficult to identify their strengths, I would say start small and be gentle with yourself. Reflect on moments when you felt confident or proud of yourself, no matter how minor they may seem. Consider feedback from others or activities where you excel. Everyone has something unique to offer, and your strengths are essential to who you are. With patience and practice, you can gradually build self-esteem and appreciate the wonder that lies within you.

RELEASE JUDGMENT AROUND OUR LOOKS

Let's face it, ladies. We're caught in the trap of comparing our looks to others. Who's prettier, thinner, buffer, sexier? It's a never-ending cycle that does nothing but bring us down.

But here's the thing, my fabulous friend: There is no such thing as "more beautiful than you" or "more attractive than you." I've been out with women whom society may deem more attractive than me, yet I've never had any trouble attracting men who find me irresistible. Beauty truly is subjective, and it's time we acknowledge this truth.

So, let's put an end to this tiresome comparison game. The people who are meant to be in our lives, whether as friends or lovers, will fall head over heels for our qualities. Forget what those glossy magazines and Photoshopped social media posts tell you. The truth is, "more attractive than you" is a myth.

This approach is an easier-said-than-done business because we've been conditioned to believe that our self-worth is tied to our appearance. When you fall in love with yourself, when you embrace your "you-ness," you won't judge yourself based on other people's opinions—and that's when you'll attract folks who love you just as you are.

HOW TO PUT AN END TO COMPARISON

It's going to take discipline and awareness to reprogram your brain to operate in a healthier and less competitive way. But fear not, my fierce friend, because I've got some tools that can help you. Here are the Confused Girl's commandments:

1. STAY A STUDENT

Imagine you're in a serene yoga class, and you're determined to conquer the twisty bird of paradise pose. As you struggle to find your balance and grace, you can't help but notice the person next to you is flowing into the pose with ease and confidence. Instead of succumbing to despair and thoughts of inadequacy, seize this moment. At the end of class, approach that awe-inspiring individual and ask for their guidance. By seeking advice, you're not saying you're inferior or admitting defeat. On the contrary, you're demonstrating a willingness to learn and improve, which is a testament to your strength and determination. You're also collaborating, right? You're connecting with someone and expressing appreciation for what they do well. Release the grip of your ego and the false narrative it weaves about your self-worth. Remember, you never truly lose; you acquire valuable lessons along the way.

Take a moment to reflect on the countless situations in which you could be learning from others and expanding your horizons. Rather than allowing comparisons to hinder your progress, become a student and challenge yourself to approach these situations with an open mind and a thirst for knowledge. Take the opportunity to learn from those who excel in areas where you may struggle. By doing so, you will not only enhance your skills and abilities but also break free from the shackles of negative thought patterns and behaviors that no longer serve you.

Next time you encounter comparisons, dare to shift your focus from comparison to learning. Growth and transformation occur through these moments of vulnerability and openness.

2. SAY SO LONG TO EXCUSES

First things first, let's address the fact that making excuses for why someone else has something you don't have is a complete waste of your precious energy. Why spend your time and effort coming up with reasons to justify someone else's success when you could be focusing on your own path? It's time to stop playing the victim and start taking control of your destiny.

By finding excuses for not having the life you desire, you're essentially giving yourself permission to stay in one place. *I can't have what I want because I live too far away. I don't have the experience. I don't have enough money. I'm bad with numbers. I don't have the time.* Those are just excuses, my friend. And excuses won't get you anywhere. There's more than one way to blaze a trail.

Let's take a look at a hypothetical to illustrate my point. Imagine your friend Olivia is absolutely killing it in the real estate game, while you recently faced the unfortunate circumstance of getting fired from your job. Naturally, money becomes a concern, and you start feeling sorry for yourself. You find yourself thinking, *Oh, Olivia's only successful because her dad is a big-time agent with a ton of connections. Nobody has ever helped me. I have to do everything on my own.* Sure, maybe Olivia did receive some help along the way, but here's the thing: It's none of your business. Remember the wise words of my dad, Giuseppe: "Stay in your lane." Instead of dwelling on Olivia's supposed advantages, focus on your own path and what you can do to achieve your goals.

Not taking responsibility for your life drains your power. Believing you're a victim and making excuses for why others are successful while you're not making the grade takes away your sovereignty and diminishes your inner strength. It's funny how we tend to throw away our responsibility when times get tough, only to reclaim it when things are going well. But here's the truth: Misfortune happens to everyone. It's a part of life.

Rather than believing that things are happening to you, see them as happening *for you*. Ditch the excuses and start taking charge of your destiny. Quit wasting your energy by comparing yourself to others and start focusing on your own journey. Remember, you have what it takes to create the life you desire. No more excuses. Put on your diamond-studded crown. Own your greatness!

3. ACCEPT THE TRUTH

There will always be someone deemed "bigger" or "better" according to our culture's ever-changing standards. One moment, it's all about being a blonde bombshell with a slim figure; then suddenly it's about being a brunette with a voluptuous derriere. And let's not forget the constant flip-flopping between small and big boobs, super fit and super curvy. But here's the thing: It's all a load of BS. Back in my high school and college days, the "it" girls were Britney Spears and Paris Hilton, epitomizing the blonde and skinny ideal. So, I rejected the appeal of my Mediterranean hourglass figure. I used to hide my hips and thighs under baby-doll dresses. Now? I proudly flaunt my sexy curves in body-hugging dresses whenever I get the chance.

The same goes for success. Society loves to put labels on what it means to be successful. If you have a big corporate job with a fancy office, you're deemed successful. But wait, then you're working for "the man," and that isn't cool. Success changes to being an entrepreneur, having your own business, and being your own boss. But wait, then you're working all the time, and you need to start implementing Tim Ferriss's *4-Hour Workweek* so you can optimize your success. It's a constant back-and-forth.

And don't even get me started on the expectations around relationships and family. Women are only deemed successful if they get married and have kids. I see so many videos on social media pitting motherhood against being child-free, and it's just not fair. Success doesn't have to be one or the other. It's about figuring out who you are and living in your truth. I'm happy being single and child-free at this time in my life, but I also understand that could change for me. I might find happiness in being married with a kid someday. Let's not back ourselves or others into a corner. Life is about going with the flow and discovering ourselves in the process. And that truth is personal to each of us.

So, let's break free from the ever-changing pressure of trends and societal expectations. They're like waves in the ocean, always shifting. But your personal truth—your understanding of beauty, success, individual choices, and worthiness—is yours and yours alone. It's about celebrating your unique qualities, knowing that your worth is not defined by external standards or comparisons to others. Let's focus on our personal truth, our inner qualities, and our own path to happiness. That's where real beauty and success lie—within ourselves.

4. BE HONEST WITH YOURSELF

There will never be another *you*. No one else possesses your soul or brings what you offer to the world. It's time to connect with the innate wisdom within.

We must love ourselves for who we are and not allow some

faceless marketers to convince us we desperately need improvement. They're just trying to sell us more stuff. They'll tell us that we need the latest antiaging cream to erase our wrinkles or that our homes are in desperate need of an overhaul with the trendiest designs. And let's not forget the relentless push to upgrade to the newest smartphone every year as if our lives depend on it. It never seems to end, does it? Let's remember that these standards are values placed on us—not created *by* us. What do you value?

You, my friend, are the flashiest fish in the pond because there is no one else like you. There is no one greater or lesser than you. You are simply incomparable. Why waste time and energy trying to fit into someone else's mold? Welcome your quirks, your flaws, and your strengths. They are what make you . . . you. Doesn't that sound amazing? When you fully become who you are in body, mind, and soul, you can appreciate others for who they are too. All those competitive and insecure thoughts, those false comparisons, will fade.

Let's surrender to the fact that there will always be someone who *seems* more spectacular, but let's not forget they're measured against standards that are nothing more than artificial constructs. I know this is getting repetitive, but I want you to hear me. No one else can bring what you bring into this world. You are a force to be reckoned with, a masterpiece in your own right. Instead of feeling threatened, see everyone as their own unique work of art.

5. HAVE A LOVE AFFAIR WITH YOUR BODY

Embark on an intimate conversation with your miraculous body and take a moment to revel in its beauty. Appreciate its splendor. Maybe it's the light in your eyes, your orange slice of a smile, the way your hair cascades down your back, or your graceful fingers. Or maybe you've felt unworthy for so long you can't find anything to appreciate. Well, try remembering a compliment you received or ask a friend what feature she admires about you. (Heads up: Make sure you ask someone who genuinely supports you.)

Now let your body know just how much you adore its captivating features. Be effusive: *Oh, what stunning thighs! This butt is beautiful! I love my curves! Those are impressive biceps! My skin is so soft!* You get the idea. Then move to the things you reject about yourself and tell your imperfections you love them as well. Those imperfections that our culture deems as flaws could very well be what makes you unique. Perhaps it's the cute little birthmark on your cheek that adds character to your face, or the cowlick that parts your bangs, or the stretch marks that bear witness to the birth of your child. For me, it's my rather prominent Italian nose. I rejected my schnoz most of my life, but in the last few years, I've fallen for it. This is the Silvestre nose, which connects me to my ancestry and gives me character. It helps to make me . . . me.

If you are having trouble loving your body, whether it's your thighs, belly, or breasts, take baby steps. With a tender touch, place your hand upon the part of your body that makes you insecure and give it some extra love. For example, you can say, *My belly, I love you unconditionally.* Feel the warmth of self-acceptance radiate through your fingertips, soothing any doubts or insecurities that may have lingered. Your belly is a testament to the life you have lived, the nourishment you have received, and the strength you possess. It deserves nothing less than your utmost appreciation.

Oh, the marvels of the female body! Beyond its outward beauty, our bodies are extraordinary in all the ways they work to keep us alive and thriving. From the moment we enter this world, our bodies labor ceaselessly, constantly adapting and performing countless functions to support us. Our hearts beat faithfully, ensuring that every cell receives the vital oxygen and nutrients it needs. Our lungs expand and contract, allowing us to draw in life-sustaining air. Our digestive system breaks down food, providing us with the energy and nourishment to thrive. The reproductive system—*how incredible it is*—has the power to bring forth life. Our immune system works tirelessly, defending us against harmful invaders. And let us not overlook the immense strength and resilience our bodies possess, enabling us to achieve remarkable feats, from nurturing our loved ones to pursuing our passions and dreams. Our bodies are a love story deserving of our gratitude, care, and admiration for all they do to support us.

Here's another exercise to appreciate what the body does daily to keep you alive and healthy. Stand in front of your bathroom mirror. Take a few moments to look steadily at your face. Then gaze directly into your eyes and let free-flowing words of self-love resonate within your being. You can say whatever comes lovingly from your heart. Or try these words for inspiration: *I love you. You are a masterpiece, a unique creation that cannot be replicated. Thank you for being my vessel on this remarkable journey. I know everything about you has a divine purpose even if I don't understand it. I will stop rejecting you.* Feel the power of your words resonate through your entire being, igniting a flame of self-acceptance and gratitude. Trust the wisdom of the universe, for it has crafted you with intention and purpose.

6. BE THE BOSS OF SOCIAL MEDIA

Can we have a little chat about the wonderful world of scrolling, liking, and sharing? I'm not here to tell you to ditch your favorite platforms or exchange your smartphone for a flip model. I'm here to remind you to be conscious of how you engage with it. It's not necessarily about how much time you spend on social media; it's more about intentionality. In my experience, it's best to use these platforms with your own positive intention. Maybe it's engaging from a place of exploration, learning, or building community and support.

I understand personally the way social media can control our reality. By promoting my activewear line on Instagram and documenting my solo travels, I am now considered an influencer. The funny thing is, when I started all of this, the term *influencer* was mostly unknown. I was never trying to be one. I just fell into it when I was figuring out ways to sell my activewear without a big budget.

Instagram is an incredible tool, and it helped me launch my successful international business. So, of course, I'm grateful. However, I also understand it's a mixed blessing. On one hand, it's a fantastic way to connect with like-minded souls, showcase our lives, and even boost businesses. But on the other hand, it can be a sneaky little devil that makes you feel less than compared to everyone else's perfectly curated lives. Trust me, those pictures only capture a fraction of reality. Behind those flawless filters and carefully crafted captions is a whole lot of messy, unfiltered chaos, just like in everyone else's life.

I used to be social media obsessed. I spent countless hours mindlessly browsing. Not only was it a huge time suck, but it also stole my joy, confidence, and motivation. I was living in the virtual land of comparisons. Jean M. Twenge, physiologist and author of *Generations: The Real Differences Between Gen Z, Millennials, Gen X, Boomers, and Silents—and What They Mean for America's Future*, wrote, "Every indicator of mental health and psychological well-being has become more negative among teens and young adults since 2012," following the increased use of social media.[11]

Here's the deal: Social media is a great tool to aid your life, not to make you feel like you're missing out. If you are being present and paying attention to your feelings while using social media, you're more likely to use it with intention, and there's less threat of it sucking you in. You'll be aware of your time usage, how you use it, and how you consume information, and you can have a realistic perspective that it's not really, well, real. Pay attention to how you feel as you're scrolling. Trust your gut! If something doesn't feel right or true or helpful, it probably isn't.

Remember, behind those picture-perfect posts, a whole lot of real life is happening. The more we acknowledge the messiness, the imperfections, and the unfiltered moments, the more we can see each other through an authentic lens. There's magic there. Share your authenticity, connect with kindred spirits, discover interesting new artists and useful new products, and support each other's dreams.

Let's stay conscious of our social media habits. You're in charge.

7. BLESS THIS . . . AND THAT

Here's my absolute favorite piece of advice when it comes to neutralizing comparison: Recite the Hawaiian Huna blessing every single day. If you're wondering, *What on earth is that?* let me enlighten you. In the enchanting world of Hawaiian spirituality, when

you desire something, you bless it and the person who has it—
and then you let your thoughts of envy, desire, and craving go.[12]

Imagine this: You're cruising through a particular neighborhood or town, and there it is—the house of your dreams. It's
not just a house; it's *the* house. Instead of turning green with
envy or greedy with desire, bless that magnificent home and the
fortunate family who lives in it.

Or picture this: You're at a cocktail party, and a stunning
woman walks by. She's not just beautiful; she's radiant, and she
carries herself with a grace that leaves you breathless. Instead
of feeling a pang of jealousy, bless her stunning beauty and her
effortless grace.

Of course, this blessing isn't just limited to houses and beautiful girls. Huna can be applied to anything and everything we
desire. A dream job? Bless it. A fancy car? Bless it. A trip around the
world? Bless it. By doing this, you're smashing the old, worn-out
comparison programming of playing the victim or being eaten
alive by ravenous envy. And you're not just sitting around wish-
ing for these things to appear in your life magically. You're actively
spreading good energy to someone or something and also acknowledging that it's within your ability to have that dream manifest too.

Instead of comparison, you're instilling a shiny, new program—one that's brimming with love and infinite possibilities.
Now, tell me: Doesn't that feel a whole lot better? After all, who
wouldn't want a life filled with blessings?

8. SISTERS UNITE!

I absolutely, wholeheartedly believe that the biggest hurdle preventing women from reaching our potential is our ridiculous
competition with one another. Seriously. Ladies, it's time to put

an end to this destructive behavior. When we lift each other up, there's nothing we can't reach. If we cultivate compassion and foster a spirit of mutual support, there are no limits to what we can achieve. We have the power to create a world filled with peace and prosperity for everyone. Yes, you heard me right. We are *that* powerful!

Let me take you back to a time when I was living for two months on the Greek island of Naxos. One day, I decided to take a sailboat tour to explore some of the smaller remote islands. On this trip, I had the good fortune to meet an extraordinary woman, a neuroscientist from the Netherlands. As we sailed along the turquoise waters, we found ourselves engrossed in a conversation about female competitiveness and the constraints it imposes on women. She shared her knowledge about the unconventional social structure of the Congo's bonobos, a species of great apes.

Brace yourself because this is mind-blowing stuff.

In the bonobo world, the ladies stick together like Velcro, while the bond between the male apes is relatively weak. The bonobo females share a level of unity and teamwork that is rarely seen in the animal kingdom. Unlike many other species, where males typically dominate and compete for power, bonobo females have established a unique social order that centers around female support. These alliances serve multiple purposes, including protection against aggressive males and ensuring access to resources. Bonobo females band together when threatened. They use their collective strength to ward off potential dangers. Through mutual encouragement, collaboration, and cooperation, bonobo females rise in rank and gain influence within the community. Their societal dynamic is shaped by the power and importance of female relationships. And it doesn't stop there.

Bonobo females exhibit an extraordinary level of empathy and compassion toward one another. They share food, help groom each other, and provide one another with emotional comfort during times of distress. These acts of kindness strengthen the bonds between them, creating an unbreakable sense of unity. The strong female bonding in bonobo society also has a significant impact on the overall group dynamics. By forming alliances, females ease conflicts and maintain a more peaceful environment. This approach to social interactions sets bonobos apart from their relatives, the chimpanzees, where male dominance and aggression are more prevalent.

As my neuroscientist friend pointed out, studying bonobo females provides us with valuable insights into the potential for a more harmonious and balanced society. It reminds us of the strength that lies within female relationships and the transformative power of compassion and support. So, let's take a page from the bonobo playbook and utilize the power of female unity. By uplifting one another, we can create a world where competition and comparison are replaced with collaboration and celebration. Together, we can rewrite the narrative and redefine what it means to be strong, empowered women.

I love this quote by Princess Al Joharah Bint Talal Al Saud: "Be the woman who fixes another woman's crown, without telling the world that it was crooked."[13] To this I say, right on!

❧

We can all agree that comparisons, the destructive kind, are total joy killers. They don't do us any favors—so let's leave them behind. Who's with me on this? Instead of wasting our energy on comparisons, let's celebrate and unite behind our differences. Let's revel in our individuality and the talents that make us shine. When we stop comparing ourselves to others, we open ourselves up to a world of self-love and acceptance. My friends, let's stay in our own lanes and live life to the fullest. Because seriously, life is way too short to be anyone but unapologetically ourselves.

You, my Confused Girl, are a shining star in your own right. Bid farewell to the teeter-totter of comparison and hold tight to the exhilarating freedom of self-acceptance. Let's rewrite our narrative. Let's redefine beauty on our own terms. Let's honor and love our flaws and imperfections. Let's live in a loving world.

CONFUSED GIRL RECAP:

- Hop off that going-nowhere teeter-totter that constantly makes comparisons. The superior-inferior dynamic doesn't serve you. Break free from it, move forward, and live your life without constantly comparing yourself to others.
- Instead of allowing comparisons to use you, use them as learning opportunities. Observe what others have achieved and use these observations as inspiration to push yourself further.
- Oh, those excuses—I get it, it's easy to come up with reasons why we don't have something that someone else does. But those excuses won't get us anywhere. Put an end to them and start taking action. Stop playing the victim and be the heroine of your own story.
- You know what makes you truly special? The fact that there is no one else like you. Embrace your uniqueness

and celebrate. You are the big fish in your own pond. Swim confidently and dazzle the world.

- Show some love to your body. It's been with you through thick and thin, so have a little chat with it. Tell your body how much you appreciate and love it just the way it is. Trust me, it'll appreciate the positive vibes.

- Let's look at external influences, like social media. We all know how addictive it can be, so it's important to stay conscious of how we spend our time on these platforms. Engage with meaningful content and connect with people who inspire you. Remember, quality over quantity.

- Incorporate the Hawaiian Huna blessing into your daily routine. Take a moment each day to bless yourself, your desires, and those around you. It's like a little dose of happiness that will brighten up your day and help you attract that which you bless.

- Take a lesson from the bonobo apes. These incredible creatures support their fellow females, and we should do the same with our sisters. Lift each other up, celebrate each other's successes, and be there for one another. Together, we can create a world where women empower women.

CHAPTER 4

You Are the Goddess of Creativity

> Creativity is a way of living life, no matter
> what our vocation or how we earn our living.
> —Madeleine L'Engle

After two years of working in my family's restaurant, I was back in Los Angeles, twenty-nine, about to turn thirty years old, and still trying to find my way. It was spring, a season of hope, rebirth, and renewal. But my financial reality wasn't so robust. I was $10,000 in credit card debt after investing in my activewear business and hadn't landed a steady job that could cover basic expenses like rent and food. I'd had a couple of temporary gigs. One was as a nanny for a superwealthy couple in Beverly Hills; another was selling artisanal salts at a farmers market. Still, I was in the red.

But you never know what's around the corner—particularly, as it turns out, the corner of Lincoln and Venice Boulevard.

That's where I was filling my BMW with gas at the Chevron station when I looked up and saw a cute guy, slim, with brown hair and dark eyes, staring in my direction. I was fresh from yoga class, wearing a pair of my line's leggings and feeling sexy, fit, and flushed after ninety minutes of kick-ass asanas.

We made eye contact, and he walked straight over. I was game for a little flirtation until I noticed he was holding some kind of small electronic device, twice the size of a cell phone, and realized he had something else in mind.

"Gotta few minutes?" was his opening line. It turned out he was something called an *Uber Ambassador* and wanted to know if I was interested in being a driver for the company. He told me that if I filled out their application, I would get a fifty-dollar Visa gift card right that minute. In the next breath, he explained that he also got fifty dollars for every person he signed up.

"You don't even have to become a driver," he assured me with a wink.

My mind was already racing. "How many people do you usually sign in a day?" I asked.

When he told me that it was around ten people and he made at least $500 daily, I was on it. After I filled out the form and pocketed my gift card, I drove straight home and called a friend who worked in corporate Uber. I explained that I wanted a job as an Uber Ambassador, but not in LA where I knew a lot of people in the entertainment world, not to mention old friends from college. "It would be better," I told him self-consciously, "if it was in Orange County." OC was only about a forty-minute drive from my place.

Done! It pays to have a network of friends in various aspects of life. Not only did I manage to get rid of all my debt over the next few months—and save some money—but I was spending my days outdoors meeting dozens of buff and tanned surfers.

The moral of the story is this: When faced with challenges, the key is to think outside the box and stay open to creative solutions. Opportunities will always show up in our lives. Rather than closing off options because they don't "fit" with whatever your dream is or how you see yourself or thinking you need a permanent solution—fling open the door. Broaden your horizons. Be curious and flexible, welcome possibilities, and work with what's presented. That, my Confused Sister, is the foundation for living a creative life.

CHANGING THE GAME

In an earlier chapter, I told you about the breakdown I experienced while I was at Sundance. Tough as it was, that breakdown was a game changer. It was a cosmic slap in the face that woke me from an existence I had never questioned before—and girl, oh girl, did it unleash my inner creative goddess.

Before my awakening, I had locked away the vibrant, imaginative side of me and was convinced that I wasn't a creative person simply because I didn't fit into the narrow definition of "artist." I couldn't draw or paint like Picasso, so how could I possibly be creative? But here's the interesting part: As a child, I was a vibrant, imaginative force. I would sing, dance, write poetry, direct plays with the neighborhood kids, and even design dresses. It's funny how our childhood passions often hold the key to our adult talents, right? It's no surprise I'm here, writing this book and designing activewear. I've tapped back into that creative energy I had as a kid.

However, when I entered high school, that side of me shut down. My private Catholic school was all about focusing on college, and even as a freshman, my friends' parents were already asking me about my future university plans. I mean, come on, adults, that was a bit overwhelming! I couldn't see the value in pursuing anything creative anymore. I questioned how it would benefit my future career. At that point in my life, everything I did was purely a means to an end. I didn't do anything for the sheer joy of self-expression. I did things solely to get (what I believed was) "somewhere in life." I was always chasing after a better future that seemed forever to be out of reach. But you know what? It was all a load of rubbish. No matter what I achieved, it was never enough.

Then the cosmic slap happened, and I knew in an instant . . .

. . . ANYONE CAN BE A CREATIVE GENIUS

You don't have to create anything to be creative. Sure, you can paint a mural or write a poem, but I tell you, Confused Girl, the most creative thing you can do is stay open to the world of inspiration. Life is inherently creative, and how we choose to engage with it is a creative act. Take an accountant, for example. They may not be painting masterpieces, but they can be incredibly creative with numbers. Finding innovative ways to optimize budgets, strategize tax planning, or develop financial models requires a creative mindset. Similarly, let's consider a nurse. Their job may not involve sculpting or composing music, but they can be exceptionally creative in the way they care for their patients. From finding unique solutions to comfort someone to creatively adapting treatments based on individual needs, nurses constantly demonstrate their creative abilities in delivering compassionate healthcare.

Creativity is not limited to specific professions or activities. It's about discovering the potential for inspiration and discovering fresh approaches to whatever we are doing. So, whether you're working in a bank or driving a bus, the key is *how* you do it. We all have our own personal spark, which puts us on a unique path.

If you're telling yourself that you aren't artistic or don't have any creative gifts, let go of that delusion. There are many ways that your creativity can come out to play—it doesn't have to be artistic (though if it is, that's great!). Get cozy with exploring whatever path calls you. Whether through cooking, dancing, flower arranging, cupcake baking, pumping iron, humming a hymn, or cleaning your house—feed your inspiration. Use your personal flair to express yourself. I love this quote by Kurt Vonnegut: "Practicing an art, no matter how well or badly, is a way to make your soul grow."[14]

Being a creative genius also means looking at problems in a new way and finding unique solutions that expand your horizons. It's all about breaking free from conventional thinking and looking into innovative perspectives. Let's say you're an entrepreneur trying to come up with a solution for food waste. Instead of just focusing on the traditional methods of reducing waste in restaurants or grocery stores, you start thinking outside the box. You shift your perspective and consider the problem from a different angle. You realize that a significant amount of food waste occurs in households due to excess produce going bad. Instead of just addressing the issue at the end of the supply chain, you decide to tackle it at the source. You come up with a unique solution:

a mobile app that connects neighbors and allows them to share excess produce. This way, people can give away the fruits and vegetables they won't be able to consume—decreasing waste and creating community. Good vibes all the way around!

When you approach a problem with a fresh mindset, you're letting go of preconceived notions and exploring possibilities. You challenge yourself to think beyond the obvious and push the boundaries of what's considered normal. This shift in thinking allows you to uncover fresh insights and discover new solutions that may have been overlooked.

I find it extremely helpful to nurture curiosity and remain open. By honing these skills, we develop a creative mindset that is not limited by traditional thinking or established norms. Then we can approach problems in a unique and imaginative way, which will bring about positive change.

THE PERKS OF CREATIVITY

My friend, may I confess something to you? When I was hung up on the "hocus-pocus" of outcome, I wasn't living in the moment, which prevented me from mining what is true gold—my creative spirit. Now that I'm able to slow down and appreciate walking the path, rather than fretting over when I'm going to reach the destination, I have time to observe, appreciate, learn, and create. There are five perks I've picked up along the way that I'd like to share with you. Not all of them might feel right for you. No problem: Trust your gut reaction. Trusting your intuition is also a big part of believing in your creative spirit. Maybe try them all and then decide!

1. BE AUTHENTIC

Soon after I returned to LA, I met a couple of inspiring women who confirmed that *sisterhood is powerful!* They were already on solid ground with successful careers. One was an actress, and the other a writer. We had just bought tacos from a yummy Mexican food truck, and between bites, I was telling them how I was feeling lost. Strangely enough, I discovered that at times—like with my meditation group—it's easier to open up to strangers. There's a feeling of liberation because there are no preconceived notions or expectations. So, although I wasn't sharing my confusion with close friends and family, I felt comfortable telling these women that I hadn't a clue about what I wanted to do next in my life.

"I only know two things," I said. "The first is that I'm totally confused. And the second is that no matter what I do, I have to be completely honest and authentic about who I am. No more BS." They laughed, but in a knowing, *I get what you mean* kind of way. In LA you only need to look two feet in front of you to see the thick veneer of pretense and how far from authenticity you can get. That's when it came to me. "Hey, what if I started a blog and called it *Confused Girl in the City*? What's more authentic than *that*?" One of the women immediately checked GoDaddy, a domain registry web company, to see if anyone else had the name. It was available—and that was the start of *Confused Girl*.

My endeavor began as a vlog on YouTube, and my channel was @ConfusedGirlLA. Each week, I committed to doing something new that I had never done before; then I reported honestly about my experiences on video and the blog I created. The first thing I took on was bungee jumping off a bridge ironically called the Bridge to Nowhere over the San Gabriel River.

Believe me, I was terrified. Another week, I tried salsa dancing lessons; the next time, I took a real-deal boxing class in Venice Beach. Well, you get the idea.

On average, my vlog got twelve thousand hits a week. I didn't have any particular goal—I wasn't thinking about making money, being famous, or getting free stuff. Instead, I was sharpening my creativity by telling the truth and describing my life-expanding adventures. In the process, something else happened: I started feeling optimistic, happy with my present life, and excited about the future.

PERK: It's a fact: Being creative brings you mental health rewards. When inspiration is unleashed and we see the world as a place of possibilities, those feel-good hormones, called endorphins, are released. Not only does the creative process reduce symptoms of depression, but according to a study reported in the *International Journal of Environmental Research and Public Health* in 2021, spending time on creative goals is associated with a higher number of activated positive effects. So, what are these positive effects? Cheerfulness, enthusiasm, energy, joy, and less stress and anxiety.[15] Can't beat that!

2. BE A REBEL

As kids, we're natural nonconformists; we don't know how to be anyone but ourselves. We're born rebels. But before long, as you and I both know, for most of us, that inner freedom and self-confidence come to an end. Our parents, teachers, and, eventually, our peer group and the prevailing culture tell us what we can and cannot do. The door shuts and we get self-conscious and uptight. Expressing your creative self takes a huge hit. But you can reclaim it for yourself!

For inspiration, let's look back in history at some of my favorite art rebels—the Dadaists. These really cool artists included Man Ray, Marcel Duchamp, and Max Ernst. There were women in the movement too (although, of course, lesser known), including the German émigré Baroness Elsa von Freytag-Loringhoven, Berlin Dadaist Hannah Höch, and French Dadaists Suzanne Duchamp and Juliette Roche.

The artist Marcel Duchamp fully embodied the artistic rebellion of the Dadaists. One of his most famous pieces was titled *Fountain*, which he created in 1917. I know, you might be imagining a big gushing sculpture with water spouting into the air, but it was simply . . . a urinal. Yes, a urinal. At the time, his piece was considered shocking, scandalous, offensive, and a mockery of traditional artistic values. Initially, *Fountain* wasn't even allowed to be shown in public, but over time, it became one of the most influential and iconic artworks of the twentieth century.

Dadaism was like the rebellious troublemaker of the art world back in the early twentieth century. It was all about breaking the rules and flipping the bird to tradition. Dada artists used weird, nonsensical stuff in their work to shock people and shake things up. They wanted to mess with your head and make you question what art even meant. Duchamp's rebellious creations stretched the boundaries of what was considered art, questioned the role of the artist, and ignited heated discussions about the essence of creativity and artistic expression. He shook up the art world—and changed it forever.

PERK: Common characteristics of nonconformists include independence, a desire to challenge authority, a willingness to take risks, and a passion for turning visions into reality. If you're a rebel, you'll be the one to think of creative solutions that never cross the minds of conventional thinkers. Being a rebel with a cause can be a real confidence booster. Folks who avoid conventional boxes are more likely to get noticed and have more freedom to move through life. Give it a try!

3. BE OPEN TO NEW PERSPECTIVES AND BE CURIOUS

It's easy to stay confined to our own way of thinking based on our limited worldview. But it's also boring, right? I'm a huge believer in packing my bags and taking off to exotic places to help expand my understanding of humanity. I know, not everyone has the flexibility and ability to travel great distances, but you can look no further than your armchair or a nearby neighborhood.

If it's not your time to fly off to Bali, or wherever you dream of going, you can still immerse yourself in unfamiliar environments—whether that means seeing different exhibits at museums, walking through a forest, striking up a conversation with someone, asking questions, listening to a new perspective, or traveling out of town to explore a nearby city. I sometimes suggest people allow themselves to take a drive and get lost. Turn off the GPS!

Reading a book about different cultures can also be mind-blowing and inspirational. As you get lost in the vivid descriptions, allow your senses to soar and your imagination to take flight. Speaking of books, J. K. Rowling fueled her imagination for the Harry Potter series with memories from her travels and the folks she met along the way.

Creativity is fueled by curiosity. It's essential for the imaginative mind and the searching soul. Curiosity is also the catalyst for questioning—and questioning drives us to explore the unknown. Exploration is inherently creative. Get how it's all intertwined? So don't be afraid to ask questions (there are no "dumb" ones) or to dig deeper to get answers. Without questioning and exploration, life is stagnant—and there's nothing creative about standing in one place.

When we honor different perspectives, we're allowing ourselves to expand our horizons. It gives all our senses a chance to take in new information. If we stay open and receptive, changing our perspective can help us reconsider our set ideas and grow as human beings. Think about it . . . New perspectives are like a breath of fresh air, breaking us out of those old, tired routines. Our minds love to put things in neat little categories, but that's the kryptonite of creative living. Expansion is all about breaking free from limitations and seeing beyond labels. It's about getting curious about life, my friend. That's where the real magic happens.

PERK: Curious people live longer. A study published in the journal *Psychology and Aging*, involving over 1,000 adults between the ages of sixty and eighty-five, showed that those who were rated as more curious were also more likely to live longer.[16]

4. BE PLAYFUL

Part of being creative is a lighthearted willingness to entertain lots of different ideas and experiences—and enjoying the process. If you don't get hung up on the outcome, you can have tons of fun with all the possibilities. Sure, you can try to plan ahead, but if you have to swerve to the right or left or make a U-turn, so what? Be game! Along with this playful approach comes a sense of spontaneity. Creativity requires us to seize the moment with abandon. Sometimes the detours lead us to the yellow brick road.

Thinking about playfulness, joy, and abandon, I'm brought back to my thrilling bungee jump off the Bridge to Nowhere. That experience was not only playful but a wonderful life lesson. It taught me I was capable of going against my instincts and taking a leap of faith, even if it meant leaping off a rocky cliff. It gave me a boost of confidence and a new sense of trust in myself; it taught me simultaneously to let go and to just go for it. With that, creativity took on a whole new meaning.

PERK: Being playful means you're full of fun and frolic. By its very definition, when you're playful, you're enjoying yourself. Studies support this fact. Whether you're a kid or a creative adult, play has been shown to relieve stress, improve brain function, increase energy, and heal emotional wounds.[17] It makes total sense. Every human wants to be happy with themselves and their life. By being playful and trying new things, you open yourself to a world of possibilities, attract more joy into your life, and become a magnet for happiness.

5. BE A LITTLE MESSY

Let's put Marie Kondo's tidying philosophy aside for now and consider how a juicy mess can open your mind. Creative types tend to have cluttered workspaces, not because they're slobs, but because they're too occupied exploring the bigger picture. They know that creativity is not about perfection. So, they don't waste time getting hung up on putting their pencil back in the drawer or stacking papers into a neat pile. If you're also a messy type, you get it. But if you're a neatnik, you might be skeptical. Maybe this will convince you that it's beneficial to loosen up a bit: Research from the University of Minnesota found that folks with a messy desk, as opposed to ultra-organized types, are more likely to be creative thinkers who have plenty of intriguing ideas.[18]

My dear Confused Girl, don't waste your time feeling guilty if your desk is cluttered or your coffee table is disorganized. David H. Freedman, coauthor of *A Perfect Mess: The Hidden Benefits of Disorder*, said, "A desk that's really cluttered is efficient because you have all the stuff that's interesting and possibly useful to you right at hand. On top of that, a messy desk is really expressive, it's personalized. It happens very naturally."[19] So, don't be afraid to make a mess in pursuit of your next big idea. Let your messy side shine and allow your creativity to flow freely.

PERK: Messy people are masterminds. They're used to dealing with chaos, so when it erupts, they can step right in and offer a brilliant solution. If disorganization is your jam, you're also more likely to be laid back and chill. In addition, messy individuals often have a unique ability to think outside the box and find creative solutions to problems that others may not have considered.

LET'S TALK ABOUT THE "ZONE"

Sister, there's something I need to cop to. I can be as distractible as a puppy in a room full of toys. My flash-dancing mind makes huge leaps, and I can come up with dozens of ideas. Sometimes I'm on fire. That's all fine and good until it's time to follow through on the creative inspiration and bring those ideas to fruition. When I need to settle down, zoom in, and focus, sometimes it's not so easy.

For those times when creativity needs to be followed by execution, using a technique called "Getting in the Zone" or "Being in the Flow" has been my saving grace. This is a state of intense focus and productivity. You know you're in it because time flies and you feel content, fulfilled, and supercreative. Every element in your internal and external environment is effortlessly in sync. You're not thinking about yourself or distracted by extraneous thoughts.

I imagine many of you have had these in-the-zone experiences already, whether you know it or not. But some of you might not have experienced it yet. No worries! Here are a few exercises that can help bring you into this awesome state of flow.

Ground your body and mind. When I was living in Ubud, Bali, I had a routine I stuck to consistently. Every morning, I walked to yoga for a ninety-minute vinyasa flow class. Afterward, I headed to a café for a nutrient-packed smoothie bowl. Once I felt nourished, calm, and clear-minded, I was ready to settle down and write.

May I suggest that before getting into your creative project, you engage in some physical activity and eat a nutritious meal? Movement helps release the stress hormone cortisol from your body and gets your energy circulating. Any movement that's available to you will work. We all have different abilities, and even the smallest movement—ankle rotation, neck rolls, bouncing in place—can make a difference. Also, a nutritional meal can work wonders for your creative project. It provides the body with the energy and nutrients it needs to function at its best, enhancing cognitive abilities and focus. Additionally, a balanced diet promotes good mood and mental health. By nourishing your body, you create an optimal environment for creativity to flourish.

The last part of this grounding is to empty your mind. Close your eyes, take a few deep breaths, and let go of all the thoughts about what you were doing and what needs to be done later. When you see those thoughts come up (of course they will!), just acknowledge them with a friendly *Oh, there you are*, and send the thought off to float away on an imaginary cloud.

Now that your body and mind are cleared, grounded, and primed for letting creativity take the lead, you can enhance your soul's reception.

Set the mood. I'm not always on the road. When I'm home, I have more control over my environment. Whenever I'm writing, I play classical music in the background, burn lightly scented candles, and surround myself with objects that evoke positive emotions. I like crystals, but I realize this can be a little woo-woo for some folks. Go with what works for your mood and what you have at hand. It can be a photograph of a beloved, a seashell you brought home from vacation, a bouquet of wildflowers, or your favorite mug filled with coffee or tea. The idea is to create a sense of comfort and inspiration. Have fun with it!

Create a "wall of inspiration" (also known as a vision board). This is a highly personalized corner of your space—it could be a literal part of your wall, a corkboard, or a piece of paper that you decorate. It's meant to be a visual collage of inspiring imagery that speaks to you. I cover my wall with quotes, poems, magazine clippings, images, and reminders on Post-it notes of what I want to accomplish and how far I've already come. Your wall is *your* wall. Make it yours.

Create a ritual. Rituals are a set of actions that have special meaning to you and help you transition from one state of mind to another. They can help the mind transition by creating intention, mindfulness, and focus. Rituals have different purposes, like marking important events, expressing beliefs, or just giving structure to your day. I've developed a ritual that helps me transition into my focused state. I steep a pot of tea, stretch, and then sit quietly, making a list of what I want to accomplish in the next few hours. You can experiment until you find the ritual that suits you. It's like a little mental trick to help you get in the zone and make the most of your time.

Eliminate distractions. I put my phone on silent, close unnecessary tabs on my computer, and settle into my quiet space, where I can be fully immersed in my work without interruption. Do you have a family or roommates buzzing around? Give them a heads-up that it's your "Do Not Disturb" time. Most importantly, honor your designated time—for however long that is. It's important to keep the promises you make to yourself. I find that starting with smaller chunks of time helps build a healthy routine that I can achieve and return to.

WHAT ABOUT CREATIVE BLOCKS?

Look, let's be real here. You can put your mind and body in a receptive state and set the stage with candles, music, privacy, no distractions, and still nothing—absolutely *nothing*—arrives. The only thing you're hearing is a voice in your head saying, *I can't do this.*

I totally get it. Plenty of times, I've sat down to write or brainstorm ideas for my business, and the only thing that opens in my house is the refrigerator door. But by working through these kinds of experiences, I've been able to identify some issues that keep me stagnant. Let me share them with you in the hopes that you can avoid these creativity blockers.

Don't hang out with buzzkills. I'm a pretty open person, as you may have noticed. When I have a good idea or I'm working on something exciting, I like to share what's going on in my life. But I've learned over the years that not everyone is in my corner. Sometimes the support I'm seeking isn't returned. Now, I avoid sharing my ideas with people who only find fault or who stay neutral and blasé while I'm on fire. You know, the buzzkills. Be selective when it comes to sharing your enthusiasm—find cheerleaders and stick with folks who chant, *You go, girl!*

Don't be negative. My friend Billy reached out to me because he wanted help with marketing. I was more than happy to give him my all, but I was stopped in my tracks by his negative mindset. Even though Billy had lots of advantages—wealth, talent, intelligence, connections, and good health—all he wanted to do was focus on all the reasons his idea, and my suggestions, would never work: "I don't have the time"; "I hate the idea of speaking in public." When I suggested that traveling might shake things up, his response was, "Who's going to take care of my cat? I've done enough traveling in my life." No matter what my suggestion, it was met with an avalanche of excuses. From my perspective, I saw endless possibilities. But this experience taught me a valuable lesson: If your brain is telling you no, you'll always find reasons to fail.

Don't give up. Along the way, you'll inevitably confront bumps in the road, obstacles that may at first feel overwhelming. But you've got to keep the faith and trust the process! Keep believing in yourself and stay committed to your goals, even when things get tough. Trusting the process means believing that things will work out in the end, even if the path is not always clear or easy. This will help you navigate life's ups and downs with resilience and determination. With faith in yourself, you can overcome obstacles, achieve success, and reach your full potential.

For inspiration, here are a few examples of creative types who never gave up (I keep them on my inspiration wall as a reminder): Robert M. Pirsig's book *Zen and the Art of Motorcycle Maintenance* was rejected 121 times by publishers before it was picked up and has since sold more than five million copies. Ditto for James Joyce's *Dubliners*, which was rejected by twenty-two publishing houses, as was Joseph Heller's *Catch-22*. Oh . . . and then there's *me*! My book proposal was rejected for two and a half years before two publishers simultaneously wanted it. Whatever your project, hold steadfast in the belief that you can make it work.

ENGAGE IN POSITIVE INNER MONOLOGUES

Most of us are masters at putting ourselves down. Stop that right this minute! Switch the narrative. Our brains and bodies are always listening, so be careful what you say. Our thoughts and words can have a direct impact on our physical health. Practice positive self-talk and have an inner dialogue that makes you feel good about yourself.

You could even create your own ritual that helps you shift into a different mindset before the negative self-talk gets out of control. For example, imagine your negative thoughts are being burned away in an open fire. Create a mental image that works for you. Positive self-talk can help you believe in your creative spirit, stay optimistic, focus on execution, and boost your motivation and innovation. It's the ultimate decimator of creative blocks.

Here are some phrases you can say to yourself to help you stay creative and positive:

- All I need is within me right now.
- Today is a perfect day to make my dreams a reality.
- I can be whatever I want to be.
- My ideas are unique and worthy.
- I'm an unstoppable force.
- I have gotten through 100 percent of my days. Cheers to a new one!

It's also empowering to craft your own affirmations that resonate intimately with you. Consider writing them on colorful Post-it notes and placing them strategically around your home. This can be a gentle reminder to uplift and inspire you throughout your day.

Confused Girl, now is the time. I invite you to seize your creative spirit, no matter how unconventional it may be. Break free from the chains of conformity and move to the rhythm of your own heartbeat. Let your imagination be a wild beast. Paint with words, sculpt with ideas, dance like nobody's watching, sing like nobody's listening, and create your life like nobody's judging. With every step you take, leave your mark on this world. Create a masterpiece! Because when you truly embrace your creative energy, you tap into a wellspring of joy, passion, and fulfillment.

In the end, life is too short to simply exist. It's meant to be lived to the fullest and celebrated to the max. Take risks, try new things, and let your inner dialogue tell you the truth: *You deserve to be free.* You are a creative goddess.

CONFUSED GIRL RECAP:

- Remember, creativity is not just for traditional art-ists—it's about finding unique solutions and staying open to inspiration. Stay flexible and learn how to ride the waves.

- The perks of creativity: *Be authentic!* Stay true to who you are and express yourself creatively while releasing those feel-good endorphins. *Be a rebel!* We're all born with a rebellious spirit, but society tries to squash our uniqueness. Remember the Dadaists and think out-side the box. *Be open to new perspectives!* Traveling, exploring your own city, and reading books about different cultures expand your understanding of hu-manity and all the myriad ways you can choose to live your one precious life. *Be curious!* Curiosity fuels creativity, so never stop asking questions. Plus, curi-ous people live longer, so keep that inquisitive spirit alive. *Be playful!* Creativity is all about having fun and not worrying about the outcome—just go with the joyful flow. *Be messy!* Forget about tidying up; messy workspaces are a sign of a creative mind. It's not about perfection—it's about exploring without worrying about the small stuff.

- Tips for getting in the zone: *Clear the body* with some form of exercise to get the energy flowing, and *clear the mind* with deep breaths to set your thoughts aside. *Set the mood* with ambience like music, lighting, and objects that feel like a little slice of heaven. Create a cheerleading *wall of inspiration* to reflect your dreams and aspirations. Find your own *ritual for focus* that gets you in the groove, whether it's brewing tea, dancing like nobody's watching, or reciting Shakespearean sonnets. Make sure you're in a *distraction-free space* to create a bubble of uninterrupted sacred time to unleash your creative genius.

- Tips for creative blocks: *Don't hang out with buzzkills* but surround yourself with supportive and positive people who cheer you on. *Don't be negative* by focusing on all the reasons why something won't work but see the endless possibilities of why they can. *Don't give up!* Keep pushing forward, even when faced with obstacles.

- Engage in positive internal dialogues. Try writing your own affirmations! Practice positive self-talk to boost your creativity, motivation, and belief in yourself.

- Seize your creative spirit. Break free from conformity and let your imagination run wild. Life is meant to be lived to the fullest. Take risks, try new things, and welcome your creative energy. You deserve to be a free, creative goddess.

CHAPTER 5

Start Loving the Heck Out of Yourself

You've always had the power . . . [You] had to learn it for [yourself].

—Glinda the Good Witch

When I'm traveling, feeling bored, or just in the mood for a romantic break, I sometimes check out online dating sites. It's a way to inject some excitement into my life, engage with different individuals, and explore unique personalities. Sometimes, I reach a point where I'm tired of the same social circle and crave a bit of diversity. Other times, a hint of loneliness nudges me toward swiping. Even if the encounter turns out to be a disaster, which is often the case, I try to find a lesson from it. That's exactly what happened a few years ago after I went on a Hinge date with this guy Matt. Let me tell you, it was a real eye-opener.

After I swiped *yes* to handsome Matt snuggling his golden retriever, we texted back and forth and then spoke over the phone. At the end of our easy-breezy, five-minute conversation, we enthusiastically agreed to meet the next night for dinner. In the meantime, I allowed my mind to churn, fantasizing about how amazing our date was going to be. Girlfriend, if you're one of the many American women who also use online dating apps, you know how that goes.

I was so wrapped up in my happily-ever-after daydream that I devoted a full two hours to getting ready for our date, and by the time I left my house—hair curled, smoky-eye makeup artfully applied, and wearing a body-hugging dress—I felt like a ten.

We met in a noisy LA tapas-and-wine bar, and after nervous small talk and sips of our drinks, we finally relaxed. Still, I couldn't tell whether Matt liked me or not. At some point, he leaned across the table and moved my hair over one side of my shoulder. "You look better like this," he said. In the next breath, he told me he usually dates tall, skinny models.

The confidence I had walking out my door disappeared in a puff.

Less than an hour later, I was in my car, driving home and feeling low. All I wanted was to get into bed, stream a show, and forget the date ever happened. I dragged myself into the bathroom to remove my makeup. But then something happened that shook me out of my self-loathing. When I stared into the mirror, the reflection gazing back was *me*—Giovanna, the Confused Girl. *Wow, I look gorgeous!* I told myself. *How did I let this guy, who I don't even know and don't much like, make me feel so bad about myself?*

The emotional pain I felt because I allowed myself to be judged through someone else's eyes taught me a valuable self-loving lesson. I never want to see myself through anyone else's eyes except my own—ever again!

I'm someone who can always use a concrete reminder, not just a gentle nudge. So, I came up with this plan to remind myself about self-love. I found a picture of myself and carefully cut out one of the eyes with a pair of cuticle scissors. It sounds disturbing, but hold on. I slipped the cutout eye into a round-shaped locket, one that I had left empty in the hopes of finding just the right moment to put something meaningful inside. This eye of mine, tucked into the locket that I've worn ever since, is a constant reminder that I'm the only one who can give myself validation.

Self-love is a never-ending journey that we're all on. It's not something you just achieve one day and then you're done. It's something you have to keep working on, day in and day out. Over time, I've learned a few things about what self-love means, and I'm here to share them with you.

- I can accept my weaknesses as well as my strengths.
- I've learned to care for my emotional, physical, and spiritual needs.
- Not only am I willing to work on myself without judgment but I refuse to sacrifice my own well-being to please other people.
- I'm grateful for the challenges put in front of me, knowing they will only help me engage more fully in life.
- When I mess up (as we all do), I can forgive myself.

If you've also managed to embrace all this—then, my Confused Friend, you're practicing self-love.

A self-love practice calls on us to connect to our soul and not just our ego. It's more than just chasing after superficial rewards or seeking quick fixes. It's about diving deep into who we truly are. This means engaging in activities that reflect our essence, values, and inner wisdom rather than looking for external approval. When we tap into our souls, we start to nurture ourselves and recognize our own worth. This helps us figure out what truly makes us happy and aligns with our values so we can focus on what really matters in life.

But here's the thing: If we're not willing to let go of old habits and try new ways of handling our reactions, even a life blessed with a full plate of earthly delights won't keep us from feeling self-loathing. You may be wondering—how do you know when you're connecting with your soul versus your ego? The ego often speaks in a critical or anxious voice, constantly seeking validation from others and fearing rejection. It's that little voice that says, *You're not good enough*, or *What will people think?* On the other hand, the voice of the soul is calm, loving, and reassuring. It encourages you to be true to yourself and find joy in your own path, irrespective of others' opinions.

It's important to remember that our ego isn't the enemy; it's a valuable part of us. It can protect us and drive us to achieve great things. The key is to acknowledge it and listen to it with compassion, rather than letting it take control.

So, how can the soul and ego work together? By finding balance. When you hear your ego's voice, take a moment to understand its concerns, but then bring in your soul's wisdom to guide your actions. Instead of reacting defensively to a hurtful comment, for example, you can acknowledge the ego's pain and respond from a place of self-assuredness and inner peace.

Loving your ego means accepting it as part of your whole self but not letting it overshadow the deeper, more meaningful voice of your soul. When you achieve this balance, you can navigate life's challenges with a stronger sense of self-worth and clarity.

It took a lousy date with Matt for me to gain this powerful wisdom.

HOW DO YOU FEEL ABOUT YOU?

Self-love is much more than just feeling optimistic because, as we know all too well, happiness is transient. It comes, and it goes. Self-love is solid and lasting. It's foundational and sees us through hard times. It allows us to reach inside ourselves and trust our solutions when we're faced with challenging times. When you say to yourself, *You've got this girl*, your confidence is coming from self-love.

Dr. Jeffrey Borenstein, president and CEO of the Brain & Behavior Research Foundation, sees the whole picture: "Self-love is a state of appreciation for oneself that grows from actions that support our physical, psychological, and spiritual growth. Self-love means having a high regard for your own well-being and happiness. Self-love means taking care of your own needs and not sacrificing your well-being to please others."[20]

Gauging our level of self-love is not just about observing our happiness or confidence in any given moment; it's about understanding the depth of our relationship with ourselves. The relationship we have with ourselves is the most important one we will ever have. It is a lifelong adventure filled with growth, discovery, and transformation. This relationship shapes how we interact with the world, how resilient we are in the face of challenges, and how deeply we can connect with others.

The path to self-love is a winding road with ups and downs, detours, and moments of revelation. It requires patience, self-reflection, and consistent effort. To help guide you, I have created the Loving Yourself Checklist. My goal was to create something practical you could use to gauge and grow your self-love. It's really a mix of what I've learned from my own experiences, watching others, and realizing how crucial self-care and compassion are. Think of this checklist as a friendly tool, nudging you to remember those small but meaningful actions you can take every day to build a better relationship with yourself. By using it regularly, you can make sure you're always working on loving and appreciating who you are.

THE LOVING YOURSELF CHECKLIST

Take a look at this list. If you find yourself saying, "Oh, yeah that's me," you gotta love it—because this chapter is for you! Ask yourself, do you . . .

Hyperapologize? No need to say, "I'm sorry," if you do. (That's a joke.) You overapologize for a reason. It could be that your feelings of self-worth are shaky and you're afraid you won't be liked unless you apologize. It could mean you think you're the cause of negative things that happen. Maybe you feel like a burden to others, or you put other folks' needs ahead of your own. I get it. I used to apologize if someone bumped into me.

Or I would say things like, "Sorry I talked so much" or "Sorry if you don't understand this." Enough already!

TRY THIS: If you want to stop apologizing, a good start is to pay attention to your language—words matter. They not only affect others but resonate within us. When an apology really isn't needed, how can you communicate without defaulting to it? Let's say you forgot your notes for a meeting. You didn't cause World War III, so relax and take a breath. Instead of offering a bucketful of apologies, stay in the positivity zone. "I really appreciate your patience" is a better way to accept the situation graciously. Then share what you remember from your notes and add to your ideas by trusting your creativity.

Have a hard time hearing a compliment? Could it be that you believe you're unworthy of those nice things being said about you? If so, you're definitely not alone. Many of us struggle with this. It's like a little voice in our heads is saying, "I don't deserve this praise." To truly accept compliments, you've got to start recognizing and appreciating the beauty within yourself. And that means feeling some self-love, which, let's be real, doesn't happen overnight. So, why do we have such a hard time with compliments? Sometimes it's because of past experiences, like criticism or low self-esteem, which make us doubt our worth. Other times, we're just not used to hearing positive feedback and don't know how to respond. But guess what? You can work on this by practicing a bit of self-compassion. When you're kind to yourself, you start to see your own value more clearly.

TRY THIS: The next time you have difficulty accepting a compliment, don't criticize yourself. Instead, give yourself a big dose of self-compassion: *It's okay if I have a hard time accepting a compliment. Whatever reasons are holding me back, I'll allow myself the time I need to heal. Maybe next time, I'll be more open and be able to simply say, "Thank you."*

Tend to be a people pleaser? I used to be the High Priestess of People-Pleasing—and I had a bounty of reasons for my ass-kissing behaviors. First of all, I had a really hard time saying *no* because I worried what people would think of me. I stressed twenty-four seven over it, fearing they would think I was conceited, lazy, selfish, or dumb. In the old days, when I was just starting out on my path of self-love, I was still willing to bend over backward to make people happy—especially employers.

After I returned to LA, I was working multiple part-time jobs and hustling to make ends meet. I took on a one-day job helping an acquaintance, Emily, hand out samples of diet ice cream during a huge food event at the Anaheim Convention Center. Since I liked her and was grateful for the gig, I agreed to meet two hours early to help unload the truck. As we heaved the cold boxes, Emily confessed she was nervous. Ever ready to support to the utmost, I gave her my best pep talk and then gave the job 150 percent as a low-cal ice cream pusher. Folks were grabbing those pops by the fistful. But Emily became increasingly bossy, aggressive, and controlling, putting down my approach and insisting I be the one to restock the heavy boxes of frozen goods. My resentment was mounting.

The last straw? I had to pee. When Emily told me I'd have to wait, I said with a smirk, "Okay, I'll pee right here!" She rolled her eyes as I walked away.

Once I was in the calm and quiet of the bathroom, I called a friend. "I'm in Anaheim. Can you pick me up and I'll treat you to lunch?" Food has always been an irresistible draw for my friends. So, I walked out and didn't look back.

After the verbal abuse I experienced while working in the entertainment industry, I never wanted to feel that humiliation again. This Giovanna, the one on the path of self-love, wasn't going to take it anymore. On top of it all, this people-pleasing is exhausting mentally, emotionally, and physically.

TRY THIS: Set your boundaries. It took me a while to be clear about what I was willing to do and what I wasn't until I realized my body, mind, and emotions were giving me clues. Yours is doing the same. Don't ignore these signals. If you feel resentment, anxiety, dread, stress, depression, or exhaustion because you're agreeing to someone's request—and it's not aligned with you—that's your cue to back off. Don't apologize either. *No* is a powerful word, and you are a powerful woman. You can simply say *no* and explain that you don't feel comfortable doing it.

Take criticism too seriously? Do you remember that story about the Nordstrom buyer who shot down my activewear line? I was devastated in the moment, but I was able to shake it off. By then I had learned how to let go of criticism. Some of us are naturally more sensitive to it, and that's completely okay. Whether it's because of your current state of mind or past experiences, if criticism is messing with your self-worth, it's time to find a way to let it go. Why do we take criticism so hard? Often, it's because we internalize it, seeing it as a reflection of our worth rather than feedback on a specific situation. Maybe history has taught us to expect the worst, or perhaps we're already feeling vulnerable and criticism just adds fuel to the fire. But here's the thing: You can manage this. One effective tactic is to practice self-compassion and reframe the criticism in a healthier light.

TRY THIS: Give yourself a good talking-to. What if someone you love told you how badly they felt because they were criticized? What would you say to them to help them feel better? You'd probably try to build up their self-worth by listing all their positive attributes—smart, creative, kind, energetic, whatever. When you face criticism, give yourself the same kind of pep talk. Be generous. Remind yourself of all your good qualities. You might also consider that the person who put you down may have been in a bad mood or may not have the best judgment. Also, some criticism is helpful. If it includes a suggestion that resonates with you, then it might be worth considering. By treating yourself with kindness and looking at criticism in a more balanced way, you'll be better equipped to handle it without letting it shake your self-worth. Over time, this practice can make you more resilient and help you grow from the feedback you receive.

Identify with impostor syndrome? This is a psychological condition that makes us feel as if we don't deserve our achievements. We secretly believe we're a sham and don't think we are as competent, smart, or sophisticated as others think we are. It doesn't matter if you have won awards, have garnered advanced academic degrees, earn the big bucks, or have just won a popularity contest—if you identify with imposter syndrome, you live with the fear and anxiety that the truth of who you really are (a fake) will eventually be revealed. This is closely connected with feelings of shame as well. Remember chapter two on shame? Impostor syndrome often brings up similar emotions, making us feel unworthy and scared of being exposed.

TRY THIS: Share your true feelings with a licensed mental health practitioner or in a group therapy situation. A professional therapist can help you explore the reasons behind your syndrome and develop strategies to help you overcome it. You might also choose to seek the advice of a mentor or a trusted friend who will likely empathize with your anxiety since, at some point in our lives, about 70 percent of us experience imposter syndrome.[21]

WHAT ABOUT SELF-COMPASSION?

There I was, standing at a podium in Kraków, Poland, about to give a presentation at a blogging convention. There must have been more than two hundred people in the room, and this was the first time I'd talked about my work in front of such a big audience. Of course, I was excited and feeling honored, but I was also nail-biting nervous. Who isn't? Even Taylor Swift admits to it: "I get nervous for everything—literally *everything*."[22] So, before I got onstage, I took a deep breath and reminded myself that I have a knack for public speaking. *I can do this!* was my mantra. And it worked—I calmed down . . . until all my plans for the presentation went totally off the rails. The slides wouldn't load, the audio failed, and my carefully crafted presentation devolved into me repeating, "Oh no!" I was embarrassed, humiliated, and frustrated, and I ended up spending most of the forty-five-minute talk stumbling over my cascading apologies (yes, hyperapologies).

Walking back to my Airbnb, and for the rest of the evening, I let myself fall into a pit of humiliation and self-recrimination. *Why hadn't I prepared better? Why didn't I arrange for someone to help me with the audio and video? How could I let the presenters down like this? My reputation is ruined!*

But the next morning, with the sun shining and the bedroom curtains swaying to a warm breeze, I shook myself out of it. Everything looks different in daylight, doesn't it? Instead of dwelling on the negative, I shifted my focus to self-compassion and kindness. I still allowed myself to feel some of the disappointment and frustration, but I didn't let it define me. I didn't let it become a value judgment about who I am. I reminded myself that mistakes happen, and even the most successful individuals have faced setbacks. I saw this as an opportunity to learn and grow. "Next time," I told myself, "I'll be more prepared for potential problems."

Yes, this Confused Girl embraced her self-compassion and self-love.

Self-love is about whether we like ourselves, and it relies on our ability to find ourselves worthy. Self-compassion adds a willingness to forgive ourselves and be gentle and accepting of our errors and transgressions.

Now, some of you might be wondering, does self-compassion come out of self-love? They're definitely connected. Self-compassion is like the action, while self-love is the feeling. Think of self-compassion as the way you treat yourself kindly in everyday situations, and self-love as the deeper appreciation and respect you have for yourself.

In order to tap into compassion for yourself, do you also need to have that foundational level of self-love? Not necessarily. Sometimes, practicing self-compassion can actually lead to developing self-love. When you start treating yourself kindly, even if you don't fully love yourself yet, you create a positive cycle with your actions. You'll begin to see your own worth and, over time, build that foundational self-love. It can be easier to start with self-compassion because it's more about actions and specific moments. For example, comforting and forgiving myself after my tough presentation day. Other people might need to work on self-love first before they can truly be compassionate toward themselves. The important thing is to start somewhere and let one support the development of the other. Both are crucial for a healthy relationship with yourself.

Dr. Kristin Neff is an associate professor in the Department of Educational Psychology at the University of Texas at Austin and a pioneer in the study of self-compassion. Dr. Neff has been researching this dynamic for more than twenty years. She explains it this way: "Instead of mercilessly judging and criticizing yourself for various inadequacies or shortcomings, self-compassion means you are kind and understanding when confronted with your failings—after all, who ever said you were supposed to be perfect?"[23] Ultimately Neff's message is to remember and honor our humanness.

No one gets through life without suffering. Self-compassion can help ease the pain of our suffering, reduce its effects, and show us ways to live with acceptance. But like a muscle that needs strengthening, self-compassion requires practice. It's not something our blame-centered culture promotes.

Here are the steps I take to pump up self-compassion:

- First, I acknowledge and accept my suffering instead of avoiding it, ignoring it, pushing it away, or trying to destroy it.
- Next, I remind myself that suffering is a natural part of life, and like all things in life, it's temporary and will move on. Everything, and everyone, changes.

- Then I wish myself happiness, as well as an end to my own and our world's suffering.
- I say an affirmation. It could be *I am enough, I accept myself completely,* or *I am accepting my circumstance unconditionally.* Of course, you can create your own affirmations.
- Finally, I think of what I can do to comfort myself. It can be anything from a walk in the park to a telephone call with a trusted friend or family member.

THE PARENT TRAP

I believe every person on Earth deserves love. All we want is to be loved by our parents, to be surrounded by loving friends, and to have that one special person who will love us to our dying day. Yes, most of us want a romance like the one from *The Notebook*. So why are so many people unable to attain it? It's a cliché, but it's also true: We can't love anyone until we learn to love ourselves. What's stopping us?

It all starts with family. Whether your childhood was picture perfect or a living nightmare, I suspect there were times when you didn't feel unconditional love from your parents. Maybe the love was conditional or completely missing. To begin healing, we need to remember that our parents are human. They have feelings and emotions, along with their own struggles. More often than not, most people want to be good parents. They try not to repeat the mistakes their own mother or father made. You know that expression: *We're all doing the best we can.* Well, it applies.

Still, it's helpful to become aware of the ways we didn't receive love from our family. Maybe nothing you did was good enough. Maybe your folks were workaholics and didn't have time for you. Maybe they gave more attention to another sibling. Maybe they smothered you. Or maybe they guilt-tripped you. There are dozens of other possibilities.

Once you become aware of the deficiency, you'll need to give yourself the love that you feel you missed. With this acknowledgment comes an ability to release the story we carry around. This is connected to healing our inner child, which I talk more about in chapter nine. For now, just know it's not an overnight fix, so be patient and allow yourself the time and nurturing to feel what you need to feel. Anger, sadness, anxiety, and fear are all appropriate emotions. I've been there.

I used to be a pretty angry person. Looking back now through the lens of self-compassion, it was great that I let myself express my emotions. But after a while, I started to attach myself to the anger. I could feel it holding me back, and worse, I was making myself a victim. I constantly talked about who pissed me off: friends, colleagues, and family members, even the stranger who sat next to me on an airplane or the local café's barista. All this blaming and misery weighed me down. There was no "lightness of being" as Milan Kundera might say.

It took me several years until I was finally able to move on. I found inner child guided meditations on YouTube to be a great way to connect with little me. These meditations involve visualizing your younger self and uncovering the love you didn't receive. My younger self was angry that she didn't have a voice. Through sitting with my inner child, I was able to give that love to little me by listening to what she had to say, and I started healing those old wounds. It turns out she was a very wise little kid!

When we identify as victims and blame others for the problems in our lives, we are not being the powerful creators of our own reality. Remind yourself that now you're a grown-up. You can take care of yourself with the love and care you were missing. Don't let your childhood resentments hold you back from your fabulousness.

CHOOSING TO ACCEPT AND FORGIVE

Thankfully, in its own time, my desire to be free of these negative emotions and create the life of my dreams was stronger than my anger. I practiced self-compassion, and when I chose to forgive others and myself, self-love rushed in. The misconception about forgiveness is that once you make the choice to forgive, you won't feel rage bubbling up ever again. For instance, after yoga class or meditation, I'd be filled with the cooling breeze of compassion and forgiveness. But the next day, maybe even the next hour, I would burn angry and bitter. *How dare they do that to me!* The same old voice was running the loop.

Forgiving someone isn't a one-shot deal. It's a decision you repeatedly have to make. Now, when someone who hurt or betrayed me comes into my mind, I close my eyes, take a deep breath, and say the Hoʻoponopono mantra: *I am sorry. Please forgive me. Thank you. I love you.*[24] I also say it to myself when I feel that I've let myself down or when I'm healing with my inner child. These are the words I use, but if this language doesn't work for you, no biggie. This is an inside job, so choose any phrase that helps you feel a sense of peace, forgiveness, and freedom.

Looking at forgiveness through the lens of self-love is a blessing for both you and the other person. Holding on to anger or disappointment is like carrying a heavy backpack; it's exhausting and unnecessary. Why put yourself through that?

Forgiving others—or yourself—frees up emotional space,

allowing you to focus on joy and well-being. It's an act of self-care, a way to say, *I deserve peace.* It's not about letting someone off the hook but about releasing yourself from the burden of heavy emotions. Forgiveness clears the emotional clutter, making room for positive experiences. It helps you grow and sets a healthy example for others. You might be surprised at how much lighter and happier you feel.

Whatever method you choose, the repetition of speaking forgiveness eventually allows disruptive emotions to dissipate. I've learned that those who hurt me also make me stronger. They give me the opportunity to practice the beautiful acts of forgiveness and self-compassion. *Thank you.*

DO IT WITH AN OPEN HEART

Forgiving does not mean forgetting. Once you are aware of how certain people react or act, you can create appropriate boundaries as an exercise in self-love and protection. Maybe your boundary is to never speak to them again. That's okay as long as your intention is not to punish anyone. Revenge doesn't work. If you decide to break off contact, it has to be done from a place of love. Even if you never say another word, send them compassion and inwardly wish them well.

Part of reparenting yourself with self-love is defending and respecting yourself. You're the "parent" now. Healthy boundaries are firm. Healthy boundaries mean that if others don't respect them, you have to take further action out of love for yourself. This is a crucial aspect of self-care and personal growth. When you set boundaries, you are essentially teaching others how to treat you and making it clear which behaviors are acceptable and which are not. Establishing these limits can prevent you from being taken advantage of, protect your mental and emotional well-being, and help you build healthier relationships.

This is actually how I resolved the end of a close friendship with a girl I'll call Violet. When we met in college, we shared a lot in common. We both had parents who were immigrants, we had the same majors, and when we left school, we were very ambitious and determined to make it in the world.

Violet had lied and betrayed me by hitting on the guys I was dating or the ones I liked, but I eventually overcame it, thinking our friendship was more important. But over the years, her lies continued. After a decade of friendship, she told me she had shared my posts with *her* followers to help my activewear gain media exposure. But it wasn't true. She never shared them. I couldn't forgive her lying another time. It was also clear to me that Violet didn't want me to succeed. She didn't have my back. I was so over it.

"I'm cleaning up my own act and want to live authentically," I told her. "There's no more room in my life for people I can't trust." Violet was struck speechless by my candor. I wished her well, and I really meant it. But that was the last time we spoke.

There are times when we may decide to continue contact with people who let us down. It's a personal choice. But if that's the case, don't forget the lesson you learned and the awareness you gained—you need to hold yourself accountable. Keep your tender heart protected.

BUT . . . BOUNDARIES!

While I was living in Berlin in 2019, I had an animated neighbor, Astrid, who was a waitress and an actress and who stopped by my apartment regularly for coffee. In limited English she would talk my head off about her sister, her customers, her audition, her boyfriend, her commute. You name it, I got an earful. Initially, I was happy to listen and offer my advice about her problems. Several times she expressed her gratitude for my open-door policy, which I appreciated. It feels good to help someone in turmoil. We have all been there, and I've always appreciated the people who have been there for me.

But the tables were turned when, after a stressful day and a stolen wallet, I needed to talk to someone. The world was feeling shaky. When I knocked on Astrid's door and expressed that I was having a hard time and could use some company, she seemed annoyed and inconvenienced. Astrid welcomed me in with a sigh and heard me out, but she kept looking at her phone, occasionally gazing at me with a blank stare. Abruptly she said, "You will be all right, it's just a bad day. I have to run . . . but I'll stop by this week."

This was a great addition to an already crappy day. All those hours I had listened to her, and she couldn't be present with me for twenty minutes? Well, that was the last time I confided in her and allowed her to use me as her personal therapist.

Before I began my journey of self-love, I hung around with people like my Berlin neighbor who didn't really care about me. If I'm being honest, I didn't care much about them either. The relationships felt empty, and our encounters never left me feeling good about myself. In those days, I was a bottomless pit of neediness because my vessel of self-love was on empty. I wasn't able to receive love until I gave it to myself. When I met a friend or a romantic connection who wanted to and could love me, I rejected them and would go back to what felt familiar. Do you know the Groucho Marx quote? "I refuse to join any club that would have me as a member."[25] I could relate!

One of the biggest changes I made in my life was to drop many of these so-called "friends." Now when I meet someone, I ask myself, *How do I feel around them? Do I feel anxious? Do I feel judged? Do I feel unsafe? Or do I feel peaceful? Comfortable? Accepted? Secure?* I've since created my own club where I finally feel at ease. If you ask questions and trust your inner guidance for the answers, you will be able to choose true friends who know you, want the best for you, and accept you for who you are. In turn, your life will be filled with love for yourself, for others, and for the world. I promise you.

The more you practice loving yourself and accepting who you are, the less critical you'll be of yourself and others. Isn't that wonderful?

SELF-LOVE = SELF-CARE

Many people mistakenly believe self-care means getting monthly massages or facials, going on meditation retreats, and spending time in luxurious spas. I say *YES!* to all that, but it's not the be-all and end-all of self-care. If it were, our country would be the home to superstars of self-love since self-care is globally a $5.6 trillion industry.[26]

Before my awakening, I believed a mani-pedi and a pounding back rub were the antidotes to my pressure-cooker days. Sure, I felt better for a few hours, but now I know those treatments won't give anyone a lasting sense of well-being. They won't promote the kind of self-love that nurtures our body, mind, and spirit. The best way to show ourselves compassion and recover from anxiety, stress, and exhaustion is to commit to a healthy lifestyle. But hey, don't get me wrong. I still love to party, drink a cocktail or two, go out dancing until the wee hours, and enjoy pizza and pasta (I'm Italian after all!). And, as you know, this girl is always game for adventure. So, what's a doable solution to a healing lifestyle of self-love?

Since I'm a fun-loving human who also gets pleasure from working hard, I probably can't offer a failproof prescription for self-care—but I'm happy to share my priorities. Keep in mind that my priorities might not be your priorities. If they make sense to you, be my guest and give them a whirl.

- Make your inner truth your guidepost. It will help reduce stress, depression, and anxiety.
- If you're dealing with physical or mental health issues, don't do it alone. Seek help from a professional.
- I'm a believer in eating a healthy diet, but not by denying myself delicious foods. As long as you're strong and healthy, don't compare your beautiful body to anyone else's—offer it gratitude for doing such a good job.
- Do what you enjoy for exercise, and you'll be more likely to make it part of your daily routine. I love yoga. Maybe you dig running, pumping iron, practicing Zumba, or discus throwing—whatever gets you moving, do it.
- Finally, I'm a huge believer in getting at least seven hours of sleep nightly. Without enough z's, our brains can't function properly, and we won't have the energy to live life to the fullest. Okay, it's not always easy for me to get enough shut-eye, especially when I'm

jet-lagged, but it's definitely a priority, and I use every technique in my toolbox to make it happen. If a solid night's sleep is only a dream for you, check out these tips from the Sleep Health Foundation[27]: Invest in the right bedding so that you match your personal body temperature—if you usually sleep hot, use lightweight, breathable bedding, and if you sleep cold, get cozier materials like flannel. Block out the light. Minimize noise. Set the thermostat between sixty and sixty-eight degrees Fahrenheit. Set your alarm for the same time each day—weekends are no exception. Keep naps to no more than twenty minutes and none after 2 p.m. Relax for thirty minutes before bed. Disconnect devices in the hour before bed. Get at least thirty minutes of natural light exposure a day, and exercise at least twenty minutes each day. Limit caffeine after 2 p.m. Sweet dreams!

MAKE A VOW TO YOURSELF

The British writer and self-styled mystic philosopher Alan Watts said, "The only way to make sense out of change is to plunge into it, move with it, and join the dance."[28] That's how I look at it too. I've made a vow to myself to lovingly and kindly be in charge of my life, to take initiative and shape my world with self-compassion and self-love. I've worked on letting go of my anger, maintaining a healthier lifestyle, forgiving myself and others, reducing my habitual apologizing and people-pleasing, and being sure I'm the one in charge of how I see myself. This, Confused Girlfriend, is what I want for you.

Self-love isn't just a buzzword; it's the foundation for

everything. It's the door to every path, every dream, every relationship. Every answer to every decision is born from loving yourself. When you ground yourself in self-love, you unlock the potential for true happiness and fulfillment. You become the architect of your own life, capable of navigating any change or challenge with grace and confidence.

So, take this to heart: Love is always the answer—for you and for everyone. Embrace it, nurture it, and let it guide you. Your journey begins and ends with self-love, and it's the most powerful tool you have. Go forward with this knowledge and watch how beautifully your life unfolds.

CONFUSED GIRL RECAP:

- Even if a date is a bust, you can still get something beneficial out of it. I realized that I should never let someone else's opinion define my worth. I created a reminder of self-love by cutting out one of my eyes in a photo and wearing it in a locket. The goal is to see and validate yourself through your own beautiful eyes.

- Go through the Loving Yourself Checklist: Stop over-apologizing and start trusting your own creativity. Practice self-compassion when receiving compliments. Set boundaries and learn to say no without apologizing. Don't take criticism too seriously and remind yourself of your positive qualities. Seek professional help or talk to a mentor if you identify with impostor syndrome.

- When things don't go as smoothly as planned or when you're faced with a less-than-perfect performance, flip the script and embrace some serious self-compassion and kindness. Life always gives us an opportunity to turn things around! Self-compassion is all about giving yourself a big ole bear hug when you mess up. It's about forgiving yourself and accepting those glorious mistakes we all make. Because let's face it, we're all a little bit imperfect, aren't we?

- Truly loving others starts with loving ourselves, which can be tough if we didn't feel unconditional love as kids. By understanding our parents' struggles, recognizing how we missed out on love, and practicing self-care—like forgiving past resentments and using tools such as inner child meditations—we can heal and empower ourselves without letting childhood experiences hold us back.

- Forgiving isn't about forgetting; it's about setting boundaries to protect yourself, whether you decide to cut ties or keep some distance while guarding your heart. Acceptance and forgiveness aren't one-time things; you have to keep working on them. I've found that practicing self-compassion and using tools like the Ho‘oponopono prayer help me let go of anger and make room for self-love. It's a process, but each time I choose to forgive, I feel a bit stronger and more at peace.

- Self-care is not just about indulging in luxurious treatments but also about committing to a healthy lifestyle because let's face it, a happy body is a happy mind! Truth be told, taking care of yourself can help reduce stress, depression, and anxiety—and who doesn't want to be stress-free and fabulous? So, get your groove on by engaging in exercise you actually enjoy, get your beauty sleep, eat a healthy diet, make truth your north star, and seek a therapist or doctor if you need a helping hand.

- Make a vow to lovingly and kindly be in charge of your life, take initiative, and shape your world with self-compassion and self-love. Remember, when in doubt, love is always the answer!

CHAPTER 6

Destiny Is a Moving Target

It is a mistake to try to look too far ahead. The chain of destiny can only be grasped one link at a time.

—Winston Churchill

Just like a lot of women in their twenties who live in LA, my friend Dani dreamed of snagging the gig of a lifetime—the kind that would give her fame, fortune, free designer gowns, a mansion on the beach, and most importantly, the opportunity to do something she loves. So, Dani spent plenty of time going on job interviews, which is definitely *not* her happy place.

"I want to pull my hair out when the interviewer asks me where I see myself in five years. I want to say, *Do you know where you'll be in five years? Look, I could be married, I could have a kid, I could be single, I could move to Europe, I could be here working at your company. Hey, I could own your company. I could move back to the East Coast. Or I could be dead.*" Dani paused for a second to contemplate her last possibility—and that's when I jumped in.

"Forget five years . . . Who knows where we'll be in the next five minutes . . . no, make that seconds." It was a rhetorical question, but then—not really. I'm definitely in agreement with the spiritual teacher Eckhart Tolle who said, "Realize deeply that the present moment is all you ever have. Make the Now the primary focus of your life."[29]

EVERYTHING IS CHANGING

Let's talk about quantum physics—the study of matter and energy. From the quantum physics perspective, everything, and I mean *everything*, in our reality is on the move—vibrating, merging, separating, and, yes, changing. Everything on an atomic and subatomic level is in motion at all times. The way we see things might make it seem like they are standing still or unchanging, but in reality, at the quantum level, everything is always in motion. Imagine you're sitting in a room looking at a solid wooden table. To your eyes, the table appears completely unchanged. However, if you zoom in to the atomic and subatomic levels, you'd see that the atoms making up the table are constantly moving. Electrons are zipping around the nuclei of atoms, and the atoms themselves are in a state of constant motion, even though the table seems perfectly stationary to you. So, while our everyday perception tells us the table is solid and unchanging, quantum physics reveals that it's actually a dynamic and constantly moving structure on the atomic scale.

This is pretty heady stuff. Let's put it this way: The only thing you can depend on is change. It's the absolute one thing that remains constant. As the Buddhists know, impermanence is all we've got. So, buckle up, buttercup; let's go on a ride together and I'll show you what I mean.

From 2015 to 2017, my first two years into starting *Confused Girl in the City*, I wanted to be the next Sophia Amoruso—the creator of the Nasty Gal e-commerce site. She had opened a few stores in Los Angeles, had an office with three hundred employees, and had just come out with her hit book, *#Girlboss*. I daydreamed about walking into my own huge LA office with *five hundred* employees—all women, of course.

My Confused Girl office would have a yoga studio and yearly yoga retreats in Bali, as well as an organic café and free Confused Girl activewear for all employees, and once a week, a super inspirational speaker would fire us up with an unforgettable workshop. Every one of my super employees would be super happy, and we would all be super fulfilled women. I had this whole freakin' fantasy figured out, and it was a super one. I mean, wouldn't you want to work there?

About a year later, my perspective began to shift. Although my business was thriving with steady growth and I was finally able to live off the profits—no more part-time jobs, thank God—the fantasy of having a big office with lots of employees started to look more like a recipe for increased work and stress. At the time, I had two amazing interns who came to my house a couple days a week, and we would sit around my large dining room table and brainstorm growth ideas on my chalkboard wall. Every article of clothing was shipped from my house, and I was the one doing all the inventory and shipping.

Half of my bedroom was a packaging area. When I was traveling for my blog, my parents would stay at my place and ship the packages for me.

But as I was traveling more, I had this deep desire to leave Los Angeles and run my company from different parts of the world. I had an itch to get moving, and I was feeling it in my soul. At the same time, I fell out of love with LA. So, I decided to transition my company to a drop-shipping model. I found a company that would produce and ship clothing as orders came in. Despite my profit margins taking a big hit after hiring an intermediary, I remained undeterred. I was ready to spread my wings and fly. You know how it is when a relationship is over—how you can't force yourself back into love? Even though it would have been easier to stay on the West Coast with its sunny comfort and familiarity, we were breaking up. It was over. I was being called elsewhere.

By its very nature, jumping into the unknown can be scary—and I was scared. The ego part of me was saying, *I can't do it!* but another, more urgent part of me was crying out, *Life is an adventure. I'm with you!* That inner voice was my soul telling me what it wanted—and what my soul wants, my soul gets.

Now that's a motto to live by.

Once I accepted this, I really had no choice. I knew my life would never be authentic unless I was willing to take bold steps and walk steadily toward change. If I continued to ignore the calling from within, I was going to be glue-stick stuck to my old life, and I would be going absolutely nowhere. I started living by my motto: *What my soul wants, my soul gets.*

If you hear your soul calling and you're also thinking about changing your life, I know how hard it can be. There's even a name for it. Fear of change is called *metathesiophobia*, and it's a common experience. A lot of us fear change because it means losing control over who we think we are. This kind of fear is ego-driven. The ego never wants to lose its grip. It doesn't want our soul to take the lead. It doesn't like things to change. Maybe you're frightened about abandoning your old role. Or you're anxious about leaving home or quitting a job. Or you're worried you'll disappoint friends, family, or colleagues. Maybe you're concerned about your finances. Or you're worried you'll be all alone on your new journey.

I get it, but I'm here with you. I have your back—100 percent. If you're listening to your soul's calling and contemplating making significant changes in your life, I have suggestions to make it happen.

FOUR WAYS TO OPEN THE DOOR TO CHANGE

1. SLAY YOUR INNER DOWNER

Do I hear you saying, *This is too hard. I can't do it. I've invested so much into where I am now. I'll hurt too many people. I'll be more successful if I stay put.* Well, that's not your soul talking . . . That's your anxious ego. We all have a negative inner voice telling us things. Quiet it down and tune into your deeper self. The confident soul voice says, in a very loving but firm way, *This is your life. Only you can make your dreams come true. Follow your desire. Have faith in yourself and the universe. Be courageous. You will do this.*

2. SEEK ASSISTANCE

Of course, the number one person who needs to motivate you is *you.* But there are others around you who can also help. Whatever your dream, wherever you want to take your life, look for people who have made their dreams come true. Read books about women who have changed their lives and found true happiness. Reach out to pros who understand change, such as life coaches, therapists, and spiritual guides. Use what is available to you without shame.

3. HAVE PATIENCE

I'm not talking about procrastination. Get going, but don't expect instant results. It's not easy to create meaningful change in your life—it often takes time. Be decisive, then allow enough time for those changes to grow and emerge. If it's taking longer than you hoped or expected, investigate why. Is there something external that needs maneuvering, or is it an inside project? Sometimes we have emotional blocks that need our attention before we can move ahead. If other steps are needed to make your dream a reality, take them. Remind yourself that patience *really* is a virtue. Don't give up. Give it time.

4. SHIFT THE WAY YOU LOOK AT MONEY

Money flows in both directions, so don't cling to it fearfully or spend it without thought. When it comes to my personal finances, I always keep one hand on the steering wheel at all times. I suggest the same for you, especially if change means quitting a lucrative job. I probably wouldn't be saying this if I had Beyoncé's big bucks, but I don't. So, I developed a strategy. The first thing I do when faced with a financial decision is to look at my values. I make a list of what's most important to me and what makes me happiest. If the financial decision matches up, I feel confident spending the money. Here are my top values:

Independence. I love to have the freedom and independence

to travel, but I always do it in a financially responsible way. This usually means organizing as many collaborations as I can via my Instagram account. A collaboration is a trade. The company gives me a stay or experience, and I give them publicity on my social accounts and blog. This includes five-star hotels, tours, and dinners. I have had some of the best experiences of my life collaborating with various companies and brands. However, if I am not collaborating, I stay in a discounted Airbnb and limit how much I spend on food and everyday activities. I would love my flights to be in first class, but it's on the wish list. Someday.

Honesty. I am a truth seeker who looks for authentic relationships built on trust and transparency. This, my friend, is another expression of true freedom. When it comes to managing your finances, honesty with yourself is absolutely crucial. This means really taking a look at your financial situation, understanding your spending habits, and being realistic about your goals. If you're transparent with yourself about your income, expenses, and savings, you'll be in a much better position to make informed and effective decisions. By having honesty as a value, I make a conscious effort not to spend beyond my means. Despite the financial challenges of my profit margins taking a hit, I remained steadfast in my commitment to responsible spending and prioritized my long-term goals over short-term gains. And if you're seeking advice from financial advisers, honesty and transparency become even more important. Building a relationship with an adviser you can trust is invaluable. You want someone who's open about their fees, their methods, and the potential risks involved in different financial strategies. That way, you know they're truly acting in your best interest. To sum it all up, it's essential to prioritize honesty in our financial decisions and resist the temptation to spend more than we have.

Self-improvement. I embrace opportunities for growth in all areas of my life—career, relationships, and personal well-being. This may mean taking a workshop, going on a retreat, or visiting a sacred site. But sometimes these experiences are financially out of my reach. If that's the case, I put them on my wish list—and wait for the right time. Then I look for something comparable, such as books, YouTube videos, and articles, so I can learn and connect in a different way. The good news is that the two essential ingredients for self-improvement are free: self-discipline and courage.

Travel and personal growth are my top values when it comes to my personal finances. I make sure that I don't lose focus on my must-haves. I make a list and prioritize my spending. By doing this, I try to avoid frivolous waste and impulsive spending. Sometimes I slip up and spend too much on makeup. But by keeping priorities clear in my mind and staying within my means, more often than not, anxiety is the only thing that ends up in the debit column.

THREE OTHERWORLDLY WAYS TO OPEN THE DOOR TO CHANGE

Otherworldly is a term we use when something feels like it's from another realm, beyond our everyday experiences. It often conjures up images of the mystical, ethereal, or even supernatural. When we describe something as otherworldly, it might seem strange, magical, or fantastical—something that fills us with awe and wonder.

I'm not someone you'd call "woo-woo," but I'm also not a

complete skeptic. I'm sensitive and have always had a strong sense of intuition. Sometimes I have dreams or visions that end up coming true. It doesn't happen all the time, but when my spirit guides or higher self wants to tell me something, I usually get the message. I'm someone who likes to blend the practical with the mystical. I believe we all have the ability to tap into our intuition and understand things on a higher level. Not everyone is into looking beyond practical or psychological guidance, and that's totally okay. I just ask that you keep an open mind. I believe in picking and choosing what feels right for you. If you're open to alternative approaches, let me share a few out-of-the-box techniques that have helped me honor change and move ahead.

1. WALK THROUGH A LABYRINTH

As reported by Robert Creenan, "According to the Labyrinth Society, a labyrinth is a meandering path, often unicursal, with a singular path leading to a center."[30] It's an ancient structure dating back four thousand years or more. I think about the labyrinth as a symbolic way of walking through life. When you start, you're wondering what the point of it all is. *Why do I have to walk through a maze? Why can't I just walk directly to the center?* Then, when you are almost to the center, the labyrinth takes you all the way back to where you started. It doesn't seem to make much sense—or does it? Sometimes life takes us in surprising, roundabout routes.

While I was walking the Phang Nga Bay labyrinth in Thailand, I met an Icelandic man, Jesper, who told me he had been an ER doctor for a few years but didn't know if he could take the stress much longer. "I think about the suffering of my patients all the time. It stays with me even after I'm home, miles from the hospital," he confided. "I don't want to sound like a selfish person, but it's wearing me down, taking all the joy from my life." Then Jesper told me the reason he was traveling through Asia and walking the labyrinth. "I want to find my soul's true desire, even if it means I have to change the direction of my life."

I keep Jesper in mind when I think about my own willingness to change direction and begin anew. I also take every opportunity to walk a labyrinth if there's one to be found during my travels. There's something about the act of slowing down, being intentional with each step, and really focusing on the present moment that I find incredibly rewarding. Plus, I find it sparks my creativity. Letting my mind wander as I walk often leads me to some really innovative ideas.

If you're curious, the website labyrinthlocator.com offers a list of labyrinths all over the world.

2. SIGNS. YES, SIGNS.

After I quit the restaurant and went back to LA, I was always on the lookout for part-time gigs. At the time, I was about three months into starting my *Confused Girl in the City* blog. Money was short, so when I heard about a well-known holistic healer who had a wellness YouTube channel and needed someone to interview him, I was on it. Driving up to his house through the radiant hills of Southern California, I knew this was going to be an adventure . . . and I was right. The minute I stepped through the doorway, I felt something strange. It was as if I was home for the first time in my life—like déjà vu, the feeling that I had lived through this moment before. In only a split second, we connected deeply. We fell in love, but not in a romantic way. In my entire life, I had never had this kind of instantaneous bond. I started to weep uncontrollably.

Once I settled down, we ended up talking about everything except his healing practice. We were more interested in the paths our lives had put us on, and without having to say it, we both knew our encounter wasn't about an interviewing job. Before I left his home, he led me into a room with hundreds of crystals and told me to take my time, walk around, and choose two crystals that resonated within me.

I was drawn to two agate stones. Each was slightly larger than the palm of my hand, and both were shaped like faceted pyramids. One was hot pink, and the other was a deep-plum color. When I held them, my body was infused with a wave of joy and a subtle tingling vibration. As soon as I got home, I placed them tenderly on my dresser. That way they would be the first thing I saw when I woke in the morning.

Around two weeks later, while I was meditating on a cushion and sitting across from the dresser, I had a vision of creating a yoga-wear line inspired by healing crystals. I visualized taking photos of these beautiful, powerful crystals and printing their images onto leggings. Initially, I was simply captivated by their beauty. Their colors and textures were mesmerizing. But as I went deeper into my research, I discovered their incredible healing properties. That's when it hit me: *Every woman should be able to rock crystal leggings in her yoga class and be reminded of her power.*

That's how the idea for crystal-inspired leggings came about. These leggings aren't just a fashion statement; they're a way to set intentions and bring a sense of well-being into your everyday routine. Imagine wearing leggings that not only make you look good but also remind you of your personal goals and aspirations. Each pair is designed to resonate with the unique energy of different crystals, serving as a constant, wearable affirmation of your intentions.

And that's how my yoga-wear brand was born. It was something I never thought I would do, but I followed the signs and trusted my intuition. I paid attention to the little nudges and synchronicities that kept pointing me in this direction—starting with my encounter with the holistic healer. Whenever a new idea or opportunity related to this venture came up, I took it as a sign to keep moving forward. I listened with an open heart and took decisive action. This path has been full of unexpected twists and turns, but each sign led me to create something meaningful.

3. BE A PSYCHIC ANTENNA

In 2017, while driving my frequent route from Los Angeles to San Luis Obispo, I was mindlessly belting out Bonnie Tyler's "*Total Eclipse of the Heart*," and suddenly instead of lyrics, I heard these three words: *Write your book.* At first, I was shaken by the unexpected interruption, but then waves of energy (or excitement—however you want to think about it) were flowing through my body. *Keep your eyes on the road*, I reminded myself. But for the rest of the drive, I gave serious thought to what I had to say to other Confused Girls like me. I knew in my soul, my book had to be written.

I don't know where this voice came from, but as you can see, I listened. It reminded me of the loving voice that told me to accept my life during my breakdown. If you stay open to ideas, spoken or unspoken, that come to you, your life can change for the better. This book is a testament to it.

You see, the concept of a psychic antenna is fascinating and multifaceted, opening up a myriad of possibilities for the voice I heard. Psychic antennas are often described as an intuitive connection to higher energies, spiritual guides, or the collective unconscious. Imagine a psychic antenna as a sort of spiritual radio, tuning into frequencies that offer guidance, insights, and sometimes even warnings. When I heard the words *write your book*, it felt like a transmission from a higher self, a guardian angel, or maybe even a benevolent spirit guide. These entities or aspects of consciousness often communicate to guide us toward our life purpose, helping us align with our true path.

When that message hit me, I felt a surge of energy—like my soul was saying, *Yes, this is it!* It felt like clarity, or even validation, that I was on the right track. By staying open to these messages, you allow yourself to be a conduit for wisdom that transcends ordinary understanding. This openness can lead to profound personal growth and transformation, guiding you toward a more authentic, happy, and free life.

So, keep your mind and heart open. The universe has a way of speaking to us in the most unexpected moments, and when we listen, we unlock the potential for extraordinary change. By sharing my story, I hope to encourage you to stay attuned to your own psychic antenna. Who knows what amazing insights and opportunities you might discover?

HOW TO TUNE IN

Who can argue with what Albert Einstein said about the importance of intuition in our lives: "The intellect has little to do on the road to discovery. There comes a leap in consciousness, call it intuition or what you will, and the solution comes to you and you don't know how or why. All great discoveries are made in this way."[31]

I believe that in every moment of our lives, we receive unspoken messages that guide us in our lives. Many people naturally have a handle on tuning into these kinds of intuitive messages. They pick up on gut reactions, trust them, and then act on them. For example, you might decide to wait for the next train and end up running into a good friend. Or you may have a feeling that you shouldn't go to a particular restaurant, but you go anyway, only to discover it closed the previous week. In a survey of two thousand adults, a whopping 70 percent said they trust their instincts, and 35 percent said they experience a physical gut feeling.[32]

This is what intuitive folks say they pay attention to:

- Strong emotions that can't be explained involving people or events.
- Haunting dreams that are not forgotten for days or weeks after you've had them.
- Unexpected physical reactions such as a vibration, sudden chill, or an intense rush of energy.

Anyone can tune in to their intuition, but it takes practice to sharpen this kind of awareness. There are different techniques that can help you get there, and you can start right now.

It's essential to pay close attention to your intuition, treating it like a skill that needs to be honed. This involves training yourself to be acutely aware of what you're feeling and sensing in your body. Intuition can manifest in various ways—sometimes it's loud and clear, while other times it's quiet and nuanced.

By regularly tuning in to these subtle signals, you can develop a deeper understanding of your instincts and make more informed decisions. Here are some tips to help you become more tuned-in to what you're receiving. Choose the ones that "feel" right for you.

KEEP A DREAM JOURNAL

Dreams play out on a different plane than our waking reality. While the rational part of our brain thinks all day long, in our dream world we tune into an unfiltered source of creativity and guidance. The more you can remember your dreams and call on them to influence your waking life, the better you'll be able to tap into your intuition—and I'm speaking from experience.

I've found that the best way to remember my dreams is to keep a dream journal by the side of my bed. As soon as I wake from my dream or first thing in the morning, I write down everything I can remember. You can also draw pictures or diagrams if that's helpful. The more frequently I recall and record my dreams, the better I lean into their messages and tap into my intuition for guidance.

You can take this a step further: After writing down what the dream was about, ask yourself what you think it was trying to tell you. Look at the symbolism. Was there anything in particular that stood out? For instance, did you see specific objects, people, or places that seem significant? How do these symbols relate to your waking life? Analyze how you felt after the dream—were you anxious, calm, or happy? These emotions are not random; they are intuitive clues that your subconscious mind is trying to communicate something important. By going deeper into the symbolism and emotional resonance of your dreams, you can uncover layers of meaning that might not be immediately apparent.

This process not only helps you understand your dreams but also strengthens your intuitive abilities. Over time, you'll find that your dreams offer invaluable insights and guidance, helping you navigate your waking life with greater clarity and confidence.

ENJOY TIME IN NATURE

Several studies show that spending time in nature is a big deal.[33] It relieves stress, lowers blood pressure, enhances our immune system, increases self-esteem, reduces anxiety, and improves our mood. These beneficial reactions help us to become more receptive and open. But how does spending time outside make us more intuitive? When we're surrounded by nature, we naturally become more in tune with how we're feeling. The calming and grounding effects of being in a natural setting help quiet the constant chatter in our minds, making it easier to hear our inner voice. Being grounded means being fully present in the moment, connected to the Earth, and balanced in both body and mind. This sense of groundedness is key for tapping into our intuition because it clears away mental clutter, making space for those "aha" moments to come through.

Think about it—when you're grounded, you're better able to listen to the subtle cues from your body and mind. You become more aware of the sensations, emotions, and thoughts that pop up, providing a clearer channel for intuitive insights. This heightened awareness helps you make decisions and take actions that feel aligned with who you really are.

For *all* these reasons, get your butt outside. It's probably easier to do if you live in a rural area or by the ocean, but even if you live in a city, there are ways to appreciate nature. You can walk through a park, visit a botanical garden, stop by a river, notice your neighbor's window boxes, pause to listen to birdsong, or just look up at the sky.

STICK TO A MEDITATION PRACTICE

Our lives are busy, I get it. But, sister, if you can commit to a daily meditation practice—even if it's just five minutes a day of sitting in silence—I promise your life will change. You'll not only be more chill and less reactive, but you'll be open to your intuition. That's because meditation helps to quiet our mind and focus our attention on our soul's inner voice. You can also choose to do a daily silent, slow-walking meditation, referred to as "kinhin," which is part of the Buddhist tradition. All it takes is choosing a path, connecting with your breath, focusing on intentional steps, and paying attention to your senses and sensations. Give it a try!

TRUST YOUR BODY

According to Dr. Judith Orloff, bestselling author of *The Genius of Empathy*, our "intuition operates through the right side of our brain, the brain's hippocampus, and through our gut."[34] That's because our digestive system contains neurons similar to the ones in our brain. For me, when something is "true" or "beneficial," I feel a sense of expansiveness. If I feel clenched and closed down, I'm not receptive to the world around me. Also, my digestive system gets sluggish. During these times, I know that whatever is presenting itself just isn't right for me. Trust your gut! The next time you're not sure about a decision you have to make, try doing this body scan:

While sitting comfortably in a chair, close your eyes and take a deep breath in through your nose. Exhale fully through your mouth. Ask your question. If it were me, I'd ask, Should I travel to Greece? You probably have a different decision to make. Then, starting at the top of your head, gently scan down through your body noticing whether you're feeling expansive and light or heavy and clenched. After approximately five minutes of this quiet scanning, I bet you'll have your answer.

Fun Fact: Ladies, because of our incredible intuitive sense, intelligence agencies like the CIA know that women make excellent spies. Dr. Michelle Martin, a contributing writer for *HuffPost*, wrote that women are able to "recognize personal and social patterns that are not visible to men. Female spies are often lauded for having an 'extra antenna,' for having better people skills, for being better at reading body language and for more easily picking up on social cues."[35]

Intuition is your best resource when navigating life changes. Think of it like an internal radar, picking up on signals and giving you the clarity you need when things feel uncertain. Trusting your gut can lead you to opportunities and experiences that truly align with what you want, making the whole process of change a lot smoother and more fulfilling.

DEALING WITH OBSTACLES ON THE ROAD TO CHANGE

Let's imagine you've found the very thing that ignites your soul and you're taking the next steps to turn your dream into a reality. You are passionate, motivated, and starry eyed. Then all of a sudden, seemingly impossible obstacles rise like the Rockies, and scaling these metaphorical mountains feels overwhelming.

More often than not, these obstacles are practical problems that need solving. For example, when I came up with the idea to create an activewear line inspired by healing crystals, I met with every dye sublimation manufacturer in Los Angeles. Dye sublimation is a special type of printing used to transfer dye to fabric. If I wanted to make my crystal vision into a reality, I needed this process. But no matter how hard I tried negotiating (and I'm pretty good at talking my way into getting what I want), I couldn't find a manufacturer to make the leggings for a price I could afford. I was told that I would have to order thousands of leggings to get a profitable price. There were two big problems with this news: 1) I didn't know if I could sell even one pair of leggings, and 2) I didn't have the money to buy one hundred pairs, let alone thousands.

I was just about ready to give up on my dream.

"I can't do this, it's impossible," I whined to my good friend. "I don't understand why I was led here. It's a dead end!"

My friend is a wise woman, and we've been besties since childhood, so she knows when I've reached my breaking point. "Take the weekend off," she suggested. "Relax and don't think about it at all. You can go back to your problem on Monday. Deal with it then."

Well, I listened to her excellent advice and gave myself the weekend to not think about it. I allowed myself to unwind. Come Monday, I got an email from one of the companies I had contacted. They said they would work with me for the price I needed! *Wow. Wow. Wow.* I did a wild, happy dance of gratitude around my living room. Even better, this obstacle taught me a lesson. I learned that even though it may feel as if you've hit a brick wall, it doesn't mean it's time to give up. You have to keep the faith. At the right time, a breakthrough will appear.

An analogy I like to use is to imagine a seed being planted in the ground. The seed experiences a lot of pressure from the surrounding dirt. It takes time and a great amount of effort for it to break through the earth and make its way to the surface. However, with patience and the appropriate amount of watering, a stem rises from the ground, and in time, a beautiful flower is in bloom. When we start something new, there will be obstacles, and that's perfectly natural. All we can do is keep moving forward at the pace that works, give our dream what it needs to grow, and keep believing in the vision. I think there is a misunderstanding that if we are on the right path, everything will just flow. The flow does exist, and things may move quickly, but there will still be challenges that we have to deal with—and they may be stressful or unpleasant or may temporarily stop us in our tracks. Try not to get too discouraged. This is life.

The manufacturing experience also taught me that sometimes you have to take your foot off the pedal. You can be moving along on your path at a steady clip, and suddenly there's a sign up ahead to slow down. That's okay. Even if you have to come to a full stop, you'll get going again. When I need to reboot, I make a list of everything I've accomplished so far and give myself credit. I also allow my fair and sensible inner critic to evaluate how I can improve my situation. Sometimes that requires patience; other times, it might mean changing direction.

I didn't create my leggings, shirts, beanies, sports bras, and swimsuits all at once. I started out with three pairs of leggings, and then I grew to six pairs and then nine pairs. This went on and on for five years until I had built up a diverse collection of products. If you are moving forward, a little bit each day is an accomplishment. I learned how to crawl until I could walk. I walked until I could run—and now I'm running until I can fly.

CELEBRATE SMALL WINS

Sometimes we get fixated on reaching our big goals and forget to be grateful for the less dramatic changes we've made along the way. For a long time, I didn't give myself credit for taking that job as an Uber Ambassador and paying off my ten-thousand-dollar credit card debt before the colossal interest started mounting. It also took a while to applaud myself for getting my leggings into the esteemed New Mart Building in downtown LA. This is a big deal for a designer.

The old Giovanna was quick to dwell on her mistakes and disappointments but sluggish when it came to acknowledging her achievements. Celebrating is so much more fun! Now I recognize not only my major achievements but my mini victories too. I remember my setbacks and am grateful for how they've brought me to the present. I remind myself of how far I've come—and how much my life has changed.

If there's no one around to give you a high five, give one to yourself. Even better, pat yourself on the back (it's easier). You've made changes in your life—and, sister, that's huge.

GIVE YOUR SISTER A HELPING HAND

The iconic actress Audrey Hepburn said, "Remember, if you ever need a helping hand, it's at the end of your arm. As you get older, remember you have another hand. The first is to help yourself, the second is to help others."[36]

Throughout my life, there have been people who have

helped me gain the strength, perspective, and motivation to make positive changes. This has often happened on my travels. When I arrived in Thailand, I was suffering from staggering homesickness and a broken heart. My sadness was so overwhelming that I barely noticed I was living in paradise. On a lucky day, I met a fellow traveler who told me about a Thai man named Vares who gave amazing foot massages. "Vares will change your life," she said with a voice so convincing I decided to book an appointment.

The next day, a small Thai man with a boyish build and a glimmering smile met me at the doorway of a storefront. He led me into a small airy room. Without much preliminary conversation, Vares began to skillfully massage my feet, and my body instantly relaxed. I mean, I was a lemming. After fifteen heavenly minutes, he stopped and looked up at my face. It felt like endless silence before he spoke again. "Why does a pretty girl have such sad eyes?" he asked. I was magnetically drawn to his dark eyes. They were staring lovingly into mine. Unconditional compassion began flowing through me.

I broke into tears—the kind where you hyperventilate. When I finally caught my breath, I told him about the breakup, the loneliness, the shame. "You need to strengthen your heart," he said kindly. "Meet me here tomorrow at eleven in the morning, and we will strengthen your heart."

The following day, to my surprise, Vares led me to a Muay Thai boxing facility where a seventy-eight-year-old Thai boxing champion gave me a lesson involving strong, combative swings. Afterward, I was exhausted but elated, and honestly ready to rest, though Vares had another idea. He led me once again through the streets, this time to a Buddhist temple. There, we released fish into the river while I quietly spoke my intention: *I intend to heal and strengthen my heart by finding moments of peace and solace within myself.* Then we went inside the temple, prayed, and were blessed by a monk. By the time I got back to my apartment, my heart was stronger and lighter, and in the place of sadness was an overwhelming feeling of sweet gratitude and compassion for myself.

Beings like Vares have made unforgettable differences in my life. I've never forgotten their wise words of inspiration and the literal healing they have offered. Now I feel it's my turn to pay it forward with the words in this book. My hope is that you'll do the same when you come across someone who is going through a trying time and you have some wisdom to share.

Studies show that helping others not only makes us feel good about ourselves but boosts self-esteem, creates a sense of belonging, reduces stress, and actually helps us live longer.[37]

By staying open to the signs and messages that the universe sends our way, whether they be subtle nudges or clear guidance, we can align ourselves with our destiny and create a positive impact on the world around us. By changing ourselves, we can also change the world and make it a better place for everyone. Even if destiny is a moving target—change is a great place to aim our arrow.

CONFUSED GIRL RECAP:

- Change is the one constant we are guaranteed in this life. Accept the change: Follow the calling of your soul, overcome the fear created by the ego, trust in your ability to navigate the unknown, and make significant shifts in your life. You've got what it takes, and the universe has your back!

- Four ways to help change happen: Tell your anxious ego to take a back seat, and listen to your confident inner voice, seek support from those who have succeeded, be patient and decisive in the process, and manage your money by aligning it with your values and priorities.

- Explore alternative approaches: Walk a labyrinth, follow the signs, and be a psychic antenna. Let your inner mystic lead you to infinite possibilities and adventures. Tune into your intuition and be your own badass guru. Trust those gut feelings, pay attention to haunting dreams, and embrace unexpected physical reactions. Also, you might want to keep a dream journal, spend more time in nature, meditate, and let your body be your guide. Oh, and remember, women have a supersensitive spidey sense when it comes to intuition. Trust that inner spy!

- While you're on the road to turning your dreams into reality, obstacles may start popping up. Don't fret, my friend! These obstacles are just practical problems in disguise. Take a breather, let your mind unwind, and come back with a fresh perspective. You will be amazed at how a breakthrough can magically appear when you least expect it. Keep moving forward, even if you have to slow down. Crawl until you can walk, walk until you can run, and soon enough, you'll be soaring high above those obstacles.

- Don't forget to celebrate those small wins along the way. Whether it's paying off a chunk of debt, witnessing your personal growth, or experiencing an advancement in your career, give yourself a pat on the back. Celebrate everything, from mini victories to setbacks that taught you valuable lessons. You've made incredible changes in your life, and that calls for some serious celebration.

- Remember, sis, you've got two hands—one to help yourself and one to help others. Whether it's a foot massage turned heart-healing adventure or wisdom and inspiration we receive from others, there's always time to pay it forward. Helping others not only feels good but also boosts self-esteem, reduces stress, and even helps us live longer. So, let's aim our arrow at love and make the world a better place.

CHAPTER 7

Manifesting Health and Happiness

Emotions are like waves. Watch them disappear in the distance on the vast calm ocean.

—Ram Dass

It seems like a lifetime ago when I was lying face down on my kitchen floor unable to stop crying or find enough energy to stand and take a shower. I look back on that time as the *Dark Night of My LA Soul*. It was a period in my late twenties when I was a prisoner of negative, hopeless thoughts. I believed what I was thinking—and I was thinking about all the ways I wasn't good enough.

Now before I go any further exploring the nitty-gritty of my condition, I want to let you know that the start of this chapter may be a bit darker; it may trigger your own feelings of despair. Even if it doesn't resonate with your personal experience, if you're an empath, it may still bring you down.

So, with this in mind, you can choose to read with awareness and frequently check your emotional state. Or you can just flip ahead to the "Living Like a Monk" section, which picks up at the turning point of my story. It's your choice; trust your inner knowing!

> *If you or someone you know needs support, call or text 988, or chat with a support person on 988lifeline.org here in the United States. LifeLine is also available worldwide at lifeline-international.com.*

During the time of the *Dark Night of My LA Soul*, I was the Queen of Rumination, playing a loop of repetitive thoughts and dwelling on negative feelings. I reviewed over and over again the causes of my self-loathing and what I perceived as their grim consequences. I continuously compared myself to the accomplishments of my friends and former colleagues and saw myself as a loser. I thought I was overweight and too short. I couldn't stop counting my failures, couldn't find any reason to be proud of my life, and couldn't shake myself out of it. I couldn't stop thinking about *me, me, me.*

Obsessed with my world of negativity, simple chores like washing the dishes or making my bed were overwhelming. I either couldn't sleep or I slept all day. I ate too much junk food and lost all interest in the daily activities that once captivated me, like walks along the beach or my daily high-intensity interval training (HIIT). I also lost my ability to pay attention and focus—and I didn't care. I wasn't really connecting with anyone back then. I ignored calls and distanced myself from others. Los Angeles is actually a perfect place to isolate yourself if that's what you want—neighbors aren't exactly knocking on your door. I felt incredibly alone, but honestly, I didn't want anyone around me either. I just kept to myself. Sometimes when my negative thoughts were especially loud and repetitive, I Googled painless ways to take myself out. During the worst of it, I didn't think I would make it through the night.

THE FACTS ABOUT DEPRESSION

The National Institute of Mental Health reports that around 21 million American adults, or one out of eight of us, experienced at least one major episode of depression in 2021. On top of that, depression is more common in women by a large percentage. While about 6 percent of guys were depressed that year, more than 10 percent of women were battling depression.[38]

The American Psychiatric Association (APA) describes depression as a "common and serious mental disorder that negatively affects how you feel, think, act, and perceive the world." Symptoms of depression can vary from mild to severe. The APA lists these signs:

- Feeling sad or having a depressed mood
- Loss of interest or pleasure in activities that were once enjoyed
- Changes in appetite—weight loss or gain unrelated to dieting
- Trouble sleeping or sleeping too much
- Loss of energy or increased fatigue
- Increase in activities such as fidgeting or pacing, as well as slower movements or speech

- Feeling worthless or guilty
- Difficulty thinking, concentrating, or making decisions
- Thoughts of death or suicide

To be clinically diagnosed with depression, you have to experience symptoms every day, nearly all day, for at least two weeks.[39]

FINDING MY WAY OUT

Unfortunately, I fit the bill. But what could I do? You can't think yourself out of a prison that's made of thoughts. When you're depressed, your thoughts work to convince you of your unworthiness. So, if you're depressed, or even just down, remember this: Your thoughts might not be your friend. When you are in that dark place, negative thoughts can feel like the absolute truth, and your ego can be incredibly convincing in making you believe in them. From an earlier chapter, remember the difference between your soul voice and ego voice? Your ego voice is often critical, fear driven, and harsh, whereas your soul voice reminds you of your inherent worth and interconnectedness with all life. Your soul voice speaks with compassion, understanding, and unconditional love.

I knew that I couldn't open the escape hatch myself. After a few months of barely making it through each day, I knew it was time to get professional help. On a good day, I understood that my depression wasn't a sign of weakness, but it also wasn't something I was going to just snap out of either. It was an illness that required treatment. With the right care, I hoped that I would feel better. *People do get better*, I repeated to myself like a mantra. I knew that mental health care is an ongoing process—similar to staying fit or practicing an instrument. If you don't keep doing what you need to do, you can be pulled back under. Eventually, I gathered enough energy to reach out, make that call . . . and ask for the help I desperately needed.

I turned to neurotherapy. Also called neurofeedback or electroencephalographic (EEG) biofeedback, this type of therapy uses brain-wave activity to help folks learn to modify their brain activity. In my case, I needed it to stop my relentless stream of negative thoughts. Although this therapy is still in the experimental stage, I was drawn to it because I couldn't think my way out of my predicament and because it didn't include medication as part of the treatment. What I needed was to stop my compulsive thinking. Neurofeedback regulates brainwave patterns to reduce the frequency and intensity of obsessive thoughts and anxiety. It's been a game changer for me. I'm not a doctor or therapist, and my experience with neurofeedback therapy is based on my own story. I'm only speaking for myself and not recommending this therapy for anyone else. It's important to talk to a professional to figure out the best therapy for you.

Here's how it worked: It's kind of like playing a computer game, but for your brain. During a session my brain waves were collected by electrodes that were placed superficially along my scalp. The therapist would track my brain-wave activity and give me feedback through sights or sounds. For example, I would watch a screen, and when my brain produced the right kind of waves—like beta waves—the screen got brighter. If those waves decreased, the screen dimmed. Basically, the game is giving you live feedback. I was training my brain to have more of those brighter experiences. What's really cool is how this impacts your brain function. Beta waves are tied to being focused and alert. So, by increasing these waves, my brain started working more efficiently. I noticed I could concentrate better and stay more alert, and I felt sharper overall. It's like my brain learned to get into the right gear when I needed it to, which helped me in everything from work to just feeling more present in daily life.

But there's more! Neurofeedback also helps with the fight-or-flight response. This is the body's automatic reaction to stress via the nervous system, and sometimes it can get triggered too easily or too often. By training my brain through neurofeedback, I learned to regulate this response better. My brain became more balanced and less reactive to stress. So, not only did I get better focus and mental clarity, but I also felt calmer and more in control, especially in demanding situations.

With better brain function, I developed a clearer mindset. I was able to respond with less self-criticism and became less anxious. After a couple of months, my negative thinking and ruminating were put to rest. In its place, a longing for a deeper, more meaningful, and authentic life emerged. I had taken the first step toward letting go of my ego's story. Would I eventually believe that the pain and struggle of my depression were worth it? Let me put it this way . . . YES.

DIFFERENT APPROACHES

PSYCHOTHERAPY

There are several other forms of therapy that offer treatment for depression. Here is a sampling of two popular approaches, according to the APA.

In *cognitive behavioral therapy (CBT)*, your therapist helps you learn to identify and manage negative thoughts and behavior patterns that are contributing to your depression. They'll help you identify destructive thinking, change inaccurate beliefs about yourself, as well as change specific behaviors that may be making your depression worse. They'll also help you communicate with others in more positive ways. CBT deals with your current problems, rather than focusing on issues from your past.

Interpersonal psychotherapy (IPT) is a type of treatment that has been studied for years and has been shown to be highly effective, especially when dealing with depression. Your therapist will help you to learn how to improve relationships with family, friends, colleagues, and your partner. You'll find more positive and constructive ways to express your emotions and solve your problems. IPT also helps patients resolve or adapt to life's challenges and provides support for coping with depression symptoms and stress.[40] This kind of treatment follows a structured and time-limited approach. So, if you choose it, you'll likely finish your treatment within twelve to sixteen weeks, along with developing the coping mechanisms needed to maintain your emotional well-being.

Where CBT helps you modify your thinking patterns, IPT helps you change how you relate to other people. So, if you're trying to decide which one to try, here's how they differ: CBT is all about helping you change the way you think. It focuses on identifying negative thought patterns that mess with your emotions and behaviors and then working to flip them around. It's structured and often includes homework to build skills like problem-solving. On the other hand, IPT is more about your relationships and how you interact with others. It dives into things like dealing with grief, resolving conflicts, and navigating big life changes. CBT is more about what's going on in your head, whereas IPT focuses on improving your social life and communication.

However, if you're not into any kind of formal shrinking, there are other ways to reach out for assistance. Mental health does not have a one-size-fits-all solution. Don't give up on yourself or on finding the right solution for you. Sometimes we need to try different options before finding the right one.

LOOK FOR A LIFE COACH

Life coaches don't necessarily have a degree in psychology, though they usually have some sort of certification. They aren't much concerned with the past and tend to focus on the present and future. If you're really suffering and can't make it out of the house, you might even get a coach who does home visits. A life coach can help to release you from negative thinking by giving you the ability to define your present reality and then offer you the tools to stay in the positive zone and dream about your future goals. They can help you formulate concrete next steps and support you in moving forward.

SEEK A SPIRITUAL COUNSELOR

Some religious traditions have counselors who receive special training in helping people grow closer to their spirituality and sense of wholeness. These types of counselors focus on listening to God or a higher power. Tuning into something greater than ourselves can lift the burden of self-criticism, shame, and all sorts of judgment. Spiritual counseling may or may not be your thing. I'm bringing it up because it's out there and has helped people who suffer with inner turmoil. While licensed professional counseling focuses on mental health and psychological issues, spiritual counseling may include spiritual practices such as prayer, meditation, and the guidance of scripture.

A SHOUT-OUT TO EFT

According to Roberta Ndlela of the *Speaking and Communicating Podcast*, "Tapping, or EFT [emotional freedom techniques], is a mind-body therapy that draws on the traditional Chinese medicine (TCM) practice of acupuncture. It involves tapping key acupressure points (acupoints) on the hands, face, and body with your fingertips while focusing on uncomfortable feelings or concerns, and using positive affirmations to neutralize those feelings."[41] The organization EFT International offers a free tapping instruction manual on its website, and YouTube has many "follow along" examples of how this modality works. But if you're seriously considering this technique, it's best to do it with a licensed mental health professional who has additional training and experience with EFT. That's how I did it.

MY NEXT STEPS

Once my neurotherapy sessions and EFT got me off the kitchen floor, I started watching YouTube interviews about happiness and gratitude with the likes of Eckhart Tolle, Dr. Wayne Dyer, and Dr. Joe Dispenza. Their words were revelatory to me. They spoke of how true joy was a feeling of inner peace, presence, and a deeper connection to oneself and the universe. Sure, I understood them from an intellectual perspective, but that was it. I realized that I had never really experienced the joyous emotions they were describing. I'd read about people who had reached ecstatic levels, but me?

Not yet. I told myself. *In its own time.*

In that moment I felt a bubble of energy rising from the center of my abdomen. I was infused with an electric excitement that lasted maybe a minute. According to the principles of quantum physics, remember, everything is energy in motion, and I was to learn that this physical sensation was a manifestation of that energy. It was this dynamic, quantum energy within me that would eventually enable me to reach higher.

I began to have faith that there was such a thing as a life of joy and abundance, one that was free from emotional pain and shame—and I yearned for it. I was ready to surrender everything I thought I knew, everything I thought I was, and everything I thought I should become. I sat on my bed and cried out, *Set me free! Raise me higher!*

LIVING LIKE A MONK

I knew I didn't want to slip back into my old life. Something within me had dramatically shifted. I had gone through a sort of portal from the darkest place of feeling hopeless and worthless to an inner place of light and understanding. I knew I was worthy and capable of transformation. From this place of awareness, I also knew that the same old choices I made in my daily life would have to change—the same actions bring you the same results.

My old life was filled with bad habits. I was routinely bingeing on pasta and then running down to the vending machines in my apartment complex to buy peanut butter M&M's, swallowing them by the handful and downing the colorful candies with gulps of Diet Coke. I streamed for hours, watching violent shows like *Prison Break*, *Breaking Bad*, and *The Sopranos*—nothing that enriched my spirit. I wasted time mindlessly scrolling social media, comparing myself to other people, and then letting my thoughts run in a negative loop with absolutely no control or awareness.

I wanted to change. I was a new girl with a new agenda. In order to make it happen, I became a self-ordained "monk."

According to the *Collins English Dictionary*, the definition of a *monk* is "a member of a religious community bound by vows of poverty, chastity, and obedience."[42] Monks often live in monasteries and dedicate themselves to prayer, contemplation, and work. I appreciated their commitment and dedication. I was alone and isolated too. Their peaceful presence and devotion inspired me to find solace in my own solitude. I also felt an unspoken understanding that the universe was on my side. So, I wanted to embrace monkhood in my own way, with my own Confused Girl twist.

I routinely set my alarm for seven thirty every morning. When I heard the Beatles singing "Here Comes the Sun," that was my cue to stretch and force myself to get out of bed. My next move was to shuffle into the kitchen and make a steamy cappuccino. Let's be honest here, even if I *am* a self-ordained monk, I'm useless without my morning coffee. But even making that cup of joe had a different quality to it. Similar to the ancient Japanese tea ritual involving ceremonial preparation and presentation, I was more conscious of the process of brewing my coffee and steaming the milk. I was also more aware of how lucky I was that I could afford the coffee and how privileged I was to be able to enjoy it in my beautiful home with time to sip in leisure. Instead of the old Giovanna, who pretty much multitasked everything and didn't give her full attention to anything, now I had an awareness. I was grateful. Yes, something within me had shifted.

When I was done savoring my coffee, I carefully washed the espresso machine and cup and settled in to contemplate my day ahead. Without setting a specific intention, daily rituals began to emerge in the place of my aimless old habits.

For instance:

- In the place of high-intensity workouts, I began to savor gentle stretching and a breathing-focused yoga practice.

- Rather than choose a quick slice of pizza for lunch, I planned my diet for the day and made sure it was filled with fresh, wholesome foods. Soups rich in minerals, fiber, and protein and low in fat became my staple. Lentil soup was my new go-to—and I limited those vending machine binges to PMS days.

- I looked around and saw clutter everywhere. Each day, I gathered what I no longer needed or wanted and eventually turned it over to Goodwill.

- My apartment became a haven for fresh-cut flowers. I felt renewed every time I glanced over at a bouquet or took a whiff of its fragrance.

- After four months of immersing myself in the disciplined lifestyle of a monk, I realized that true transformation comes from small consistent changes rather than drastic, unsustainable shifts. As I eased up on the rigidity of my routine, I carried with me the valuable lessons of simplicity, mindfulness, and self-care that monk life had taught me. These practices continue to guide me in finding balance and harmony in my daily life, reminding me that the path to inner peace is a journey of intention, patience, and self-discovery.

PRACTICES

Throughout the day, I also engaged in several practices. It never came from a place of *Oh, I have to do this*. Instead, I literally felt a tugging inside me. I was drawn to certain activities that were now my favorite things to do.

I'll share them with you, but, girl, I believe that finding a path is personal. What appeals to me might not hold any interest for you. This is my road map, *not yours*. If you find inspiration from it, that's terrific. If you don't, please keep going—explore what lights you up. The trip you need to take will find you and point the way. Stay open!

WRITING GRATITUDE LISTS OR KEEPING A GRATITUDE JOURNAL

I'm not alone when I say that keeping a gratitude journal and writing gratitude lists helped me to be less anxious, more hopeful, and happier. The Greater Good Science Center at the University of California, Berkeley "studies the psychology, sociology, and neuroscience of well-being and teaches skills that foster a thriving, resilient, and compassionate society."[43] It published a paper in 2018 titled "The Science of Gratitude," which outlined several additional benefits of gratitude, such as

- more satisfaction with life
- less materialistic
- less likely to experience burnout
- better physical health
- better sleep
- less fatigue[44]

You don't have to make a big deal about your list or journal. Just sit down and contemplate what you have in your life that has given you pleasure. I confess that I'm not always filled to the brim with gratitude. Even those days when I was living as a monk, I had times when my well of gratitude was low.

Sometimes it's as simple as appreciating a rainy day. *I'm grateful for the soothing sound of rain.* Or it might be, *I'm grateful for having reliable transportation.* Or, *I'm grateful for this fresh salad.* Other times, I was more contemplative and found myself writing, *I'm grateful for my spirit. I'm grateful for this life. I'm grateful for my sorrows because they help me appreciate joy.* No judgment. Again, everyone feels gratitude in different ways for different reasons. Write what feels right.

There's a good chance that if you choose to do this, you'll feel the benefits. Try practicing gratitude for fifteen minutes a day, five days a week for at least six weeks, and according to researchers, you may see improved mental health and a positive change in mindset. Gratitude can also improve your physical wellness by not only reducing stress but also supporting your cardiovascular health.[45]

YOGA!

I don't know where to begin when I tell you how a daily yoga practice revolutionized my life. I get it if you're stuck on your Pilates class or get an energy rush from an aerobic workout or pumping iron. Sister, I've been there. And I'm not putting any physical movement down. Zumba, modern dance, kickboxing, climbing walls, jumping rope, or whatever—do it! I'm just saying that yoga brought me to another level.

I came to yoga through one of my former roommates, Britney, who had signed up for a thirty-day yoga challenge. One day she invited me to join her class. I agreed and was blown away. It was another tool that offered me a reprieve from my continuous loop of negative thoughts. The class was a type of practice called vinyasa, which means that we were seamlessly moving from one pose to another. I was definitely working up a sweat. But I was also forced to concentrate and stay in the moment. After class I felt a freedom throughout my entire being—not just my body. My mind was quiet, my anxiety was temporarily gone, and the self-hatred I had been clinging to dissipated. My body was as relaxed as a cat in the warm sunshine. I thought, *I have to do this every day.* So I did—and it worked. I became a yogi!

If you've never done yoga before, I definitely recommend it. But if you're just starting out, I suggest taking a beginner's flow class; however, there are various types of yoga you can explore to see which one fits you best. I also encourage you to think of yoga as a moving meditation. Leave any thoughts of inadequacy, competition, or pride at the door. Shut your ego down. Allow yourself to sense the freedom of nonjudgment while you're on your mat.

If it seems like yoga might be your thing, the Yoga Alliance website has listings of accredited yoga schools in your neighborhood.[46]

PRAYER

"Prayer is a lot like cognitive behavioral therapy," says Tanya Luhrmann, author of *How God Becomes Real: Kindling the Presence of Invisible Others*. "It's a way you attend to your own inner experience, let go of distracting thoughts and focus on more positive thoughts."[47]

Praying doesn't mean you have to get on your knees and clasp your palms together—though if that works for you, go for it. As a yoga practitioner, I automatically put my palms together in a gesture called "Añjali Mudrā" when I find myself silently praying or feeling gratitude. I sometimes pray with appreciation, thanking forces greater than myself for the abundance and grace I've been given. Other times, I pray for forgiveness or for a change in my present circumstances.

If you're into prayer, the important thing to remember is that there's never any shame in it. You can ask for whatever you want and do it your way, in the time and place that feels right for you. I've found that authentic prayer spontaneously erupts from a deep part of me. After I offer quiet words or desperately plead out loud, I calm down and feel a sense of peace. But as my bestie, Anna, likes to say, "You do you. I'll do me." Prayer is very personal.

GENEROSITY AND VOLUNTEERING

What this girl discovered about generosity is that it benefits both the giver and the receiver. Giving is the glue that connects us to each other. It doesn't matter if you give money, food, kindness, a listening ear, or your loving heart. Whatever you have, if you let it flow out in the world, it's a win-win. Just asking the person collecting your parking ticket how their day is going can be an act of generosity. Oprah, the quintessential gift giver has this to say about generosity: "The best gift anyone can give, I believe, is the gift of sharing themselves."[48]

Volunteering is a generous form of offering your time and service to help others. While I was at a low point in my life but gaining energy, I decided to get out of the house and help someone else. I chose to become a "Big Sister" in the Big Brothers Big Sisters of America mentoring program. I was matched with a fifteen-year-old girl I'll call Amy, who was going through a tough time with her mom—and at that point in her life, no other adults were giving her any positive reinforcement. No one offered her hope for the future. I made sure that I gave her that every time we went out. I pointed to all the amazing gifts she possessed. I told her she had what it takes to follow her dreams. I looked her in the eyes and said, "Amy, I believe in you."

Initially, I went into the experience of being Amy's big sister thinking I was going to help *her*. But it ended up being a two-way exchange. While I was spending time with my little sister, she got me out of my head and into my heart. I was my best self when I was with her. Plus, Amy showed me just how much potential I have to help other women. We were together for two years, and I still keep in touch with Amy. Knowing she's living a full life of abundance and joy makes me happy.

According to the Mayo Clinic, volunteering "improves physical and mental health, . . . provides a sense of purpose," and helps you "nurture new and existing relationships."[49] If you're interested in volunteering but don't know where to start, check out the organization VolunteerMatch—just type in your zip code and you'll find various volunteer opportunities in your community.[50]

HANGING WITH LIKE-MINDED SOULS

You know the expression "birds of a feather flock together"? It means that beings of a similar type, interest, personality, character, or other *attribute* are drawn to each other. The old Giovanna spent a lot of her time and energy trying to fit in with a flock she didn't even enjoy hanging with. I had my reasons—maybe they were famous or rich or just could do something for me. But the only thing I got out of these so-called friendships was loneliness.

Hanging out with like-minded souls creates a whole new level of connection, warmth, love, and respect. When we share beliefs, values, and a sense of purpose, we gain a newfound resonance and alignment. It's quite a profound experience. I had it, for example, when I met the healer who gifted the crystals. I felt an immediate familiarity, a sense that I'd known him before, and an instant affection. In time, I built a new community of friends, along with the folks from the meditation group. I finally had a handful of people who genuinely cared for me and supported me.

Have patience. Go to events that light you up, and open up to people. Attend workshops, join clubs, volunteer for causes that resonate with you, and don't be afraid to strike up conversations with strangers. It may take time for the new community to arrive, but they will eventually show up. Authentic connections are worth the wait, and every small effort you make will bring you closer to finding your people.

If you're traveling a path of growing and learning and reaching for your higher self, then I predict you'll not only meet like-minded souls but also weed out false friends along the way. This process might feel lonely or challenging sometimes, but trust that it's part of your journey toward a more fulfilling and harmonious life. With an open heart, stay true to your values and passions. The right people will recognize your authenticity and be drawn to your light. Keep nurturing those connections, and soon you'll find yourself surrounded by a supportive and loving community that uplifts and inspires you.

❧

Remember to be kind to yourself as you walk toward the light. It has taken me a decade to reach the healthy and positive state I am in today. Gradually, you will experience improvement, with shorter and less intense lows and longer and more uplifting highs. Moments of joy will outweigh despair, and you will possess a toolbox ready to confront any challenges that cross your path. When I look back over the last ten years, I'm amazed at how much has changed. Thinking about that younger version of myself, I can't help but feel a lot of compassion and admiration for everything it took to get to where I am now. All those struggles, the perseverance, and the little victories have made me a stronger and wiser person. And since I've been through this kind of growth once, I know I've got the tools and strength to handle whatever comes my way from here on out.

As you move forward, keep in mind the importance of manifesting health and happiness in all areas of your life. Picture the positive changes you want to see and take intentional steps to make them happen. Celebrate your progress, no matter how small, and be kind to yourself when things get tough. One day you will look back at you now with a big, loving, compassionate smile.

It just happens like that.

CONFUSED GIRL RECAP:

- Depression is a tough and serious condition that affects your emotions, thoughts, and actions. You might feel really down, lose interest in things you once enjoyed, notice changes in your appetite and sleep, feel constantly tired, or even have thoughts about death or suicide. It can touch every part of your life, including your relationships, work, and overall happiness. But here's the good news: Depression is something you can beat.
- Overcoming depression can take many different paths.

For me, seeking professional help and neurotherapy led to a deeper and more authentic life. Talking to a mental health professional can be a game changer, and two treatment options are cognitive behavioral therapy (CBT) and interpersonal psychotherapy (IPT). Alternative approaches might include working with a life coach or spiritual counselor or engaging with EFT. It's super important to remember that you're not stuck feeling this way forever. With the right support and treatment, many people not only get through depression but also come out of it stronger and more self-aware. Going through this can teach you valuable skills and help you build a more fulfilling life. So yes, you can beat depression and come out even better, ready to thrive and enjoy life more fully.

- Living like a monk for a time may help connect you with your true self and establish new patterns in your life. Embracing gratitude, coffee rituals, fresh flowers, and mindful habits brought me into deeper spaces of self-awareness. You can be as regimented as you'd like! The key is to establish some practices that you maintain for a set time. The more you enjoy them, the better they'll stick. New habits and routines can form anywhere from a few weeks to a couple of months.

- Practices for manifesting health and happiness: gratitude lists, yoga sessions, heartfelt prayers, acts of generosity, and hanging with like-minded souls for a dose of self-care and connection! Find the practices that spark your heart.

CHAPTER 8

Less Clutter, More Clarity

When we clear the physical clutter from our lives, we literally make way for inspiration and "good, orderly direction" to enter.

—Julia Cameron

In the eighties and nineties, during the era of neon colors, cassette tapes, and hair bigger than life, I found myself navigating the world of consumerism on steroids. My dear mother adopted the philosophy of "more is more" with gusto. A trip to the store with Mom meant entering an avalanche of potential purchases, where every aisle held a treasure waiting to be added to our already overflowing collection of stuff.

Our kitchen (*oh, the kitchen*) was a sight to behold. It was a heap of culinary contraptions, each serving a specific and often obscure purpose. From lettuce dryers and garlic crushers to popcorn makers and fondue sets, along with an ice cream maker that saw more dust than action, there was no kitchen gadget my mom didn't own. The sight of her kitchen inventory was enough to send me into a frenzy of anxiety and a longing for a simpler existence.

As I navigated through the cluttered spaces of my childhood home, I realized that less was truly more. That's why, when I moved into my own apartment, I practiced conscious minimalism. It didn't take much effort. It just seemed a more practical approach to life. More stuff just meant more to clean and take care of. It felt burdensome.

Although I tried to keep objects to a minimum, after ten years of living in the same apartment, I looked around with a critical eye and realized even I had accumulated a decade's worth of crap, stuff I rarely or never used. Since I was going to be living abroad for two years to write my book and subletting my apartment to tenants while I was away, it seemed like the perfect time to dig in and declutter. With a determined spirit, I sifted through my possessions, giving away some of my belongings to friends and donating a bunch. The rest I condensed into a few boxes and stored in my parents' garage.

I left in 2018, carrying just a backpack and one suitcase. Living with only essentials was a transformative experience—a liberating way of shedding layers of unnecessary baggage both physically and emotionally. Every new purchase I made while traveling was met with the ritual of giving away something else that I had been carrying around. Not only did this practice make room for the new belongings in my suitcase, but I also considered it a symbolic gesture of letting go—a way of making space for new experiences.

In a world where more is often mistaken for better, I learned that the true richness of life lies in the freedom of simplicity, in the joy of letting go, and in the lightness of being unburdened by excess. I returned to the States with a newfound appreciation for the beauty of less. The clutter of consumerism has never again held me captive.

WORK TO DO

Even though inheriting Grandma's china may not spark joy for millennials and younger generations as it did for our parents, we still have a long way to go in fully embodying minimalism. Minimalism has become a trendy topic of conversation these days. While society is becoming more conscious of the harmful effects of overconsumption on ourselves and the environment, the constant push to buy, buy, buy remains ever-present.

Marketers are experts at bombarding us with enticing advertisements that whisper, "This dress is adorable. Buy it and you'll be irresistible!" or "Imagine how sensational that dining room table will look at your next dinner party!" The pressure to keep up with the latest trends and products is relentless. This persistent pursuit is deeply ingrained in our cultural value system, which tries to program us to value a life full of the latest stuff and a certain model of living. This model doesn't necessarily include or respect the diversity of individual lifestyles, pushing everyone toward a homogenized ideal that may not resonate with personal values or unique ways of life.

There's also plenty of societal pressure, especially with social media blasting our friends' latest wins. Our thinking might go something like this: *Jennifer just got a new BMW, and we have the same job. I deserve one too, but maybe a Porsche will be better.* This applies to travel, beauty products, experiences, home goods, things for your kids, you name it. The urge to impress and keep up can feel like a brutal buying competition. It's a bottomless pit of desire.

The Christmas lights competition in my childhood neighborhood perfectly illustrates my point. We lived on a corner lot with a large yard and two huge trees. During the Christmas season, crowds drove through our neighborhood to see the elaborate displays. While my mom decorated the inside of our home, my father's job and joy was to take care of the outside lights.

After my father meticulously strung lights around the whole house, our neighbor added a big Santa Claus to their front yard. My father and the neighbor had an unspoken competition, so my father went to the store and bought two large angels. In turn, our neighbor bought a big blow-up snowman. What was next? My dad hired a guy to string lights on our tall trees.

My father was content because he ended up winning the competition. But here was the Catch-22: Now he was expected to put on the same light show every year. What began as a joyful display of festive spirit turned into a stressful and expensive burden driven by excess. My point is not to say don't buy a nice bag or don't go Christmas crazy on your home. But if you are expecting these things to fill some void within you, you will always be frustrated and dissatisfied with life. The mindset of "more is more, and less is never enough" will leave you disappointed, confused, and anxious.

CLUTTER = ANXIETY

After my minimalist thinking rubbed off on my mom, even the acknowledged Queen of Clutter came to see how accumulating stuff added to her anxiety. I remember when she decided to downsize after my father passed away. It was a big decision for her to sell our family home and move into a smaller, more manageable place. I was out of the country at the time and secretly grateful that I missed out on the chaos of going through all our family's belongings. But Mom told me that clearing out the house and sifting through our possessions made her realize how much stuff she had accumulated. "There was so much I never used," she admitted. It was a tough time for Mom, but also a period of sincere reflection and growth. Her new space is smaller and more serene. Now when I visit, I can exhale, and Mom is also calmer with less clutter around her.

It's been my experience that when I'm visiting a home filled with clutter, I pick up on a sense of chaos and find it challenging to focus and think clearly. I get itchy and anxious and can't wait to leave. I'm not alone. A study conducted by UCLA's Center on the Everyday Lives of Families found that the more stuff people have in their homes, the more stress and anxiety they experience. The clutter and disorganization in their living spaces contribute to an overall negative impact on their mental well-being.[51] Reflecting on my experiences, I realize how transformative it is to practice minimalism and declutter our lives. It's not just about creating a cleaner space; it's about fostering a clearer mind and a more peaceful heart.

NEVER ENOUGH?

Just like the example of my dad and the Christmas lights, the need to keep up with societal expectations can lead to a never-ending cycle. If you're busy focusing on what you don't have, you'll never be grateful for all that you possess. In my opinion, this is one of the worst feelings a human can have: the inability to feel satisfied and grateful.

In today's society, consumerism is often viewed as a modern-day religion, with material goods serving as its false gods. People are constantly urged to worship at the altar of the latest products, believing that happiness and fulfillment can be purchased. Even with technology, the pressure to upgrade and keep pace with the new creates a sense of unease and restlessness. Research has shown that individuals who prioritize experiences over possessions tend to report higher levels of happiness and well-being.[52] By focusing on meaningful experiences rather than the latest iPhone or newest sneaker drop, we make room in our being to cultivate a sense of fulfillment and contentment that's not dependent on external possessions.

The whispers of regret on your deathbed will not be about missed shopping opportunities or leaving your car behind. Instead, most people at the end of their lives express a much deeper sense of what's truly valuable in life. According to Bronnie Ware in her book *The Top Five Regrets of the Dying*, these are the kinds of longing that are most often voiced:

1. "I wish I'd had the courage to live a life true to myself, not the life others expected of me."
2. "I wish I hadn't worked so hard."
3. "I wish I'd had the courage to express my feelings."
4. "I wish I had stayed in touch with my friends."
5. "I wish I had let myself be happier."[53]

Ultimately, true fulfillment lies in the intangible moments and connections that enrich our lives beyond material possessions. The laughter shared with loved ones, the unspoken understanding between friends, and the peace that comes from living authentically create a mosaic of a life well lived. These are the legacies that endure long after the fleeting glitter of wealth and status has faded away.

HOW TO SIMPLIFY YOUR LIFE

You know how we sometimes hold on to things really tightly? Our emotional attachment to objects often ties back to memories and feelings, making us feel safe and grounded in an ever-changing world. Think about a childhood toy or a piece of jewelry from a loved one. These items aren't just things; they're symbols of significant moments and people. They help us feel connected to our past and our identity.

But clinging to things can be a sign of deeper issues like anxiety or unresolved emotions. Our belongings can act as a shield, giving us a sense of security and stability. So, when we decide to clean out a closet, it's not just a physical task; it can bring up a lot of emotions. Each item we pick up can trigger memories and feelings, making the process emotionally challenging. Even though letting go of certain possessions can feel like parting with pieces of ourselves, it can also be liberating. By decluttering, we make room for new experiences and growth. We learn to find security *within ourselves* rather than relying on external objects. In the end, understanding our emotional attachment to objects means being kind and introspective. It's about exploring our deeper feelings, acknowledging our vulnerabilities, and making way for change. This can help us build a healthier relationship with our possessions and, more importantly, with ourselves.

I am trying to take the words of First Lady Eleanor Roosevelt to heart: "A little simplification would be the first step toward rational living."[54]

If you're wondering how to simplify your life, here are some tips that have worked for me.

DEDICATE AN "I DON'T NEED IT" DAY

Apply the divide-and-conquer approach to decluttering. Instead of tackling everything at once, take it step-by-step; break up your efforts by dedicating one day a week to decluttering. Set the mood with a cup of tea and your favorite playlist. Simplifying your life should be an enjoyable process. I began with my dresser, drawer by drawer, asking myself, *Do I use this? Do I need it? Does it make me happy?* Next, I moved to my closet, breaking it down into sections. I use the two-year rule. If I haven't worn something in the past two years, out it goes. Letting go of unnecessary possessions is the first step toward a minimalist lifestyle.

THE RITUAL OF PARTING WITH SOMETHING WHEN BUYING SOMETHING NEW

I found great joy in practicing this ritual during my two years abroad. It's a habit I've carried forward. Whenever I purchase something new, it comes with the understanding that I will then gift or donate something I already own. This creates constant flow and balance. For instance, recently I bought a new pair of shoes and gifted my other nearly new pair to the wonderful woman who cleaned my hotel room. It's fulfilling to brighten someone's day with a surprise gift. This practice helps maintain balance while avoiding unnecessary accumulation.

TEMPORARY VERSUS PERMANENT

When I want to experiment with a different look, rather than invest in new clothes I might only wear once, I use platforms like Rent the Runway, Nuuly, Armoire, Nordstrom Trunk Club, and Gwynnie Bee. They offer a convenient way to play with new styles without wasting a ton of money or stuffing your closet. The same principle applies to other areas of life. Instead of buying new kitchen appliances that might only get used a few times, I use services like Cort or Wonderchef to rent high-quality gadgets and tools whenever I need them. For yard work, rather than cluttering your garage with equipment you rarely use, you can opt for tool rental services from Home Depot or local community tool libraries. By focusing on temporary over permanent, we can enjoy access to top-notch items when we need them without the burden of ownership or the waste that comes with it.

SIMPLIFY YOUR SANCTUARY

When I returned to my LA apartment after two years abroad, I found most of my furniture trashed by the renters. I knew it was time to update. Luckily, my awesome friend and neighbor, Evelyn, who happens to be a celebrity interior designer, took on the challenge of giving my place a makeover. With a tight budget, I couldn't afford to splurge on all-new furniture. So, Evelyn and I got creative and decided to decorate using leftovers from her clients' fancy mansion.

Living in LA has its perks since wealthy folks are often eager to part with their luxury items; I only had to cover the delivery fee. We snagged a custom-built couch that Evelyn had made years ago for a client. With some new fabric and cushions, this $8,000 couch ended up costing me $900. We repurposed the leftover fabric for the drapes and even scored a free beveled mirror from Craigslist. I also got a custom dining set and chandeliers from Evelyn's other clients. For every new piece we brought in, we passed on an old one that was still in pretty good condition to friends or donated it to Habitat for Humanity.

Evelyn taught me how to create a harmonious and well-organized living space by following minimalist design principles. Think clean lines, neutral colors, and comfortable furniture that promotes a serene atmosphere. We opted for functional and essential furniture pieces that create a sense of peace and tranquility. By keeping surfaces clutter-free and embracing a simple, clean aesthetic, we highlighted my crystal collection. Now, stepping into my home feels peaceful and calm.

BE A CONSCIOUS CONSUMER

Have you ever bought something only to regret it a few days later? I've fallen into that trap more times than I'd like to admit. Next time you're about to swipe that card, take a moment to ask yourself if the purchase will add value to your life. Avoid impulsive buys and stick to things that really resonate with your priorities and needs. It's important to regularly check in on your goals to make sure your lifestyle aligns with what truly matters to you.

It's important to note *why* you're buying something. You can splurge on a nice bag and feel like a million dollars every time you use it—and that feeling could last for years. The key here is spending money on what you value. The catch, though, is that cultural pressure and marketing may lead us to think that we value something that we really don't. Here are a few tips and reminders of what we've already discussed in previous chapters. The goal is to get clear on what you value and want to spend your money on.

- *Reflect on past purchases:* Look back on previous purchases and assess which ones brought you lasting joy and which ones you regretted. This can help you identify patterns and understand what truly adds value to your life.
- *Define your priorities:* Make a list of your top priorities and values. Whether it's health, education, travel, or quality time with loved ones, knowing what matters most to you can guide your spending decisions.
- *Set clear goals:* Establish short-term and long-term financial goals. When you have clear objectives, it's easier to resist impulsive buys and focus on what will help you achieve those goals.
- *Avoid social comparison:* Be mindful of the influence of social media and peer pressure. Just because everyone else is buying the latest gadget or fashion item doesn't mean it's right for you.
- *Test the waters:* If you're unsure about a purchase, give yourself a cooling-off period. Wait a few days before making the purchase to see if you still feel the same urgency or desire.

Minimalism is all about intentional living and focusing on what brings you happiness and fulfillment. For instance, if you tend to splurge-shop like my mom used to, set a monthly budget and expense limit to avoid going overboard. Make sure that staying within your budget is your number one priority.

WASTE LESS AND LIVE GREENER

Confession: Before traveling to Indonesia, I didn't grasp the whole plastic problem, and I found the mounting environmental fears like climate change annoying. I think a lot of people feel this way but are hesitant to admit it. It's easy to just throw stuff away when you don't have to look at your trash—literally and metaphorically. The United States does a pretty good job of hiding our waste, making it easy to overlook the impact of our habitual disposals. But when I lived in Indonesia, I got a firsthand look at the plastic problem.

Back in the day, Indonesians relied on bamboo and other natural materials instead of plastic. Bamboo was a part of their daily lives for centuries. It was used to make everything from household items to buildings. Its versatility and eco-friendly properties made it a popular choice well before plastic took over. Indonesians valued bamboo for its ability to be reused, recycled, and decomposed—unlike plastic. But sadly, plastic became the go-to because of its convenience, cost-effectiveness, and modern appeal. Not surprisingly, this shift has resulted in a significant environmental crisis in Indonesia. What struck me the most was seeing plastic pollution even in the remotest and most beautiful places. Rivers in Indonesia have become pathways for plastic waste to reach the oceans, causing marine pollution and harming ecosystems. Just a quick Google search of "plastic island" will show you the magnitude of the problem we're facing, and it's a responsibility we all share.

Small changes can make a big difference for the environment. Consider swapping out single-use items like plastic bags and water bottles for reusable alternatives like totes and refillable water bottles. And don't forget to reuse and recycle whenever you can. Additionally, think about buying secondhand items, combining new purchases with used ones, and recycling furniture. By giving a second life to preloved items, we reduce the demand for new resources and minimize waste. By adopting mindful consumption and making sustainable choices, we're not just helping the planet but also inspiring others to do the same. When we reduce waste and embrace sustainability, we're protecting our environment for future generations. Let's take care of the Earth and ensure it remains beautiful and healthy for years to come.

DIGITIZE AND DIGITALLY DECLUTTER

Can we just take a moment to be grateful we no longer need a million photo albums to remember all our special moments? Just thinking about it brings me gratitude for my iPhone and iCloud. The beauty of today's world is that we can shrink a whole filing cabinet into organized folders on our laptops. Let's use this technological leap and scan those paper documents, photos, and physical items to clear up space and declutter our lives!

Digitizing is a blessing for saving physical space, but our digital footprint also requires maintenance and intention. Digital clutter can build up faster than you may think! Because we can't see it around us, it tends to get unwieldy quickly—think of your inbox and all those unread emails. Start by cutting ties with unnecessary subscriptions, mailing lists, and apps. Simplify your inbox and cut down on the distractions caused by marketing emails. Forgotten subscriptions throw money to the wind. You may be surprised by how many subscriptions we unknowingly pay for without reaping the benefits. I recently reviewed all my subscriptions and discovered I had been shelling out $19.99 a month for Adobe Illustrator for a year without realizing it. I used it to digitally sign a couple of documents and for editing some PDFs, but then I just forgot I had it—and continued paying. I probably used it fewer than ten times. *Canceled!* Apps like Subscription Manager or Cancel Subscriptions are a convenient way to stay on track with all your subscriptions and expenses.

The other day, I took a deep dive into my phone apps, bid farewell to the unused ones, and neatly organized the rest into folders: *travel, communication, lifestyle, entertainment, business,* and *fitness.* Now, whenever I glance at my phone, I feel a sense of calm and order. If I had known how refreshing this would be, I would have done it ages ago!

TRIM YOUR CALENDAR

Back when I was deep in the entertainment industry, I used to boast about my jam-packed social calendar filled with after-work drinks, parties on Friday and Saturday nights, and the obligatory Sunday brunch. Looking back, it all seems like a whirlwind of busyness. I remember feeling pressure to show up at every event, even when my gut was screaming at me to just stay home. I remember one evening I was totally exhausted, but my friends insisted I join them for a night on the town. While my car was stopped at a light, I was hit from behind and had to deal with whiplash for two weeks. Anytime (and it's much less frequently these days) I ignore my inner voice, I end up regretting it.

Now that I'm a bit older and hopefully a bit wiser, I've shifted my focus to prioritize activities and commitments that bring me joy and fulfillment. I've traded in late nights at LA bars for investing in travel experiences, and I've learned to make time for those who uplift me rather than drain my energy. Also, solo evenings at home have become blissful moments of quality time with *myself.* It used to be a source of guilt if my social calendar wasn't overflowing, but now I take pride in the "less is more" approach.

I've come to understand the value of quality over quantity in all aspects of life. Learning to say no to obligations that don't align with your well-being—physically, mentally, and spiritually—is a game changer. Choose what's best for you and surround yourself with people and situations that nourish your soul. So, remember, prioritize yourself and your happiness above all else. A minimalist calendar is a lesson in self-care and self-love worth embracing.

COLLECTING EXPERIENCES... NOT STUFF

Back in high school, I was all about possessions—I was voted as the most fashionable, and I chased after the coolest cars, the latest makeup, and the big brand names. I was in a self-propelled race to have the best of everything. But you know what? As I've grown older, I understand those things might give me a quick thrill, but the feeling fades fast. I can appreciate luxury and expensive stuff, but if I were to lose them, it wouldn't shake me up. Because at the end of the day, I'm not defined by what I own.

These days, I'm all about investing in experiences that leave a mark on my heart. I'd rather drop money on living in a foreign country for a month, immersing myself in a different culture, than on a designer bag. Through my travels, I've met some incredible souls who have become like family to me. The memories we've shared, the wisdom we've exchanged—they're priceless. I've even gone back to visit some of these friends, turning them into lifelong connections scattered across the globe.

Traveling, embracing nature, and cherishing quality time with loved ones—that's where I find fulfillment and forge meaningful bonds. I believe the essence of life is nothing you can hold in your hand. Simplifying your life is getting clear on what's really valuable; it's about stripping away the noise and distractions to focus on what truly matters. When you prioritize these genuine experiences and connections, you realize that the most significant aspects of life are not material possessions but the moments and relationships that enrich our souls.

SURRENDER TO SLOW LIVING

I enjoy the art of slow living. This is my way of life! That's why, when I travel to a new place, I choose to spend at least a month there, allowing myself to adjust, explore, and be immersed in the local culture without rushing around. Even when I'm home in LA, I make time to cherish moments by taking a leisurely pace and savoring life's simple joys. Some days are easier than others, I know! But it's the intention that counts.

Once a week, I dedicate a veg-out day to simply unwind, wherever I may be. I watch Netflix, order in food, and chill. Slow mornings are my favorite as I ease into the day with a cappuccino in silence or with relaxing morning music. But if you don't have the luxury of being able to take this kind of time—I get it, life moves fast—there are other slow-living habits you might want to try, such as slowing down while you're eating and savoring every bite. Or taking a moment to look out the window at the clouds passing. Or filling in a crossword puzzle or reading a poem—all of which ask your mind to slow down and focus. There's a quote credited to Lao Tzu, the philosopher who wrote the foundational text of Taoism, that I hold dear and often reflect on when I feel the urge to hurry through life: "Nature does not hurry, yet everything is accomplished."[55]

It's time to step out of the constant hustle and focus on what truly matters: our health, peace, and overall well-being. The craving to constantly do more and tick off tasks from our list is draining. The mindset of "the more I do, the better I feel" can lead to stress, illness, and burnout. That's why Italy, with its cultural expertise in slow living, is one of my favorite destinations. Life is simpler there, with no one rushing through meals or conversations. It's no surprise they boast one of the highest life expectancies. Let's follow their lead and embrace a slower, more mindful approach to life. Let's savor each moment, prioritize presence over productivity, and incorporate the essence of slow living into our daily routines.

REDUCE MINDLESS YAKKING

Last but not least, who also has the gift of gab? The number one complaint my teachers had about me was that I talked too much in class. In our Italian Irish household, talking was encouraged—the more chatter, the better. But as I ventured outside our home, I realized that excessive talking could sometimes rub people the wrong way and lead to my oversharing. For those of you who, like me, have the gift of gab, here are two simple tips to help you navigate conversations with more intention.

Practice active listening and ask questions. When you speak less, you naturally listen more to what others have to say. By asking questions and showing genuine interest, you can learn a lot from people and better understand who you want to connect with in a meaningful way.

Take a breath and pause before speaking. This simple step

can help you gather your thoughts instead of rambling or giving away too much information. We've all been there—replaying conversations in our heads and cringing at things we wish we hadn't said. Let's avoid that self-torture.

I found listening more and speaking less uncomfortable at first, but it led to a valuable realization about myself. I discovered that when I stopped filling the silence with words, I could connect with others on a deeper level. I also learned the importance of balance in conversation—sometimes the most powerful thing you can do is simply listen. Let's embrace mindful communication and make every conversation count. You've got this!

FINALLY . . .

Living clutter-free is all about introducing simplicity to every part of our lives. It starts with recognizing where we can streamline our daily routines. This self-awareness kick-starts a positive transformation, making room for clarity to shine through. Make it a habit to find joy in simple, quiet everyday moments and cherish the peace, contentment, and gratitude they bring. As you embark on this journey toward a more minimalist and fulfilling life, remember to appreciate the beauty of living with less and connecting in deeper ways with the world and people around you.

It can take time to adjust to different ways of life, but simplifying is a lifelong practice you return to. It's often not about the things themselves but more about your attachment to them and what they represent. It's a slow peeling back and letting go. Allow each small step to bring you closer to a life filled with meaning and purpose. By trying out some of these practical tips in your daily routine, there's a good chance you'll end up paying more attention to what you're doing and may end up having a deeper appreciation for your experiences. So, Confused Girl, join me (and my mom) on this quest for a life of less.

Remember: True wealth lies in the freedom of simplicity, the liberation of letting go, and the lightness of being unburdened by excess.

CONFUSED GIRL RECAP:

- Remember how my mom embraced minimalist thinking and downsized after my dad passed away? She realized how much stuff she had accumulated and how it added to her anxiety. A UCLA study found that more stuff leads to added stress and anxiety. Decluttering isn't just about a cleaner space; it's about a clearer mind and a more peaceful heart.

- Societal expectations can trap us in a cycle of never feeling satisfied. Focusing on what we lack keeps us from appreciating what we have. Consumerism pushes us to chase the latest trends, but research shows that experiences bring more happiness. Common regrets at the end of life aren't about missed purchases but about overworking, not living authentically, not expressing feelings, losing touch with friends, and not allowing happiness. True fulfillment comes from meaningful connections and moments, not material goods.

- Decluttering your life can be a joyful and insightful practice. It's liberating to release old parts of yourself to make room for new expressions. Start by dedicating an "I don't need it" day to declutter a little at a time. Enjoy the process with tea and music while asking yourself, *Do I use it? Do I need it? Does it make me happy?*

- Be an intentional consumer. Make a habit of giving away something whenever you buy something new. Not only does this bring joy through giving or donating, but it also helps maintain balance by preventing unnecessary accumulation. Instead of purchasing clothes you'll only wear once or items that will end up gathering dust, consider using rental platforms. This way, you can access high-quality items when you need them without the hassle and expense of owning them.

- Conscious consumption and sustainable choices are excellent for both you and the environment. Give your sanctuary a makeover on a budget by repurposing furniture. Choose essential pieces that create a peaceful atmosphere and keep surfaces clutter-free. Before making a purchase, ask yourself if it would truly add value to your life. Stick to what aligns with your needs to avoid regretful buys. Reduce waste by swapping single-use items for reusable ones and recycle whenever possible.

- Digital life can be a game changer when it comes to clearing out all that paper clutter. Say goodbye to piles of files and boxes taking up valuable space in your home. But let's be real, digital clutter is a whole other beast. It's time to get your digital life in order! Sort through those apps and documents, label your files clearly, and say goodbye to any subscriptions or apps that are just taking up space. Streamlining your digital world will make everything easier to find and create a sense of calm and order.

- Invest in experiences that leave a lasting impact rather than chasing material possessions. Collect memories and forge meaningful connections. Trim your schedule to prioritize activities that bring you joy and fulfillment. Say no to obligations that don't align with your well-being. Slow down and savor life's simple joys. Listen more. Take time to appreciate each moment and prioritize your health, peace, and overall well-being. Inhale before speaking—a big breath—so that you share valuable insights instead of later regretting what accidentally flew out of your mouth.

CHAPTER 9

Decoding Romantic Relationships

Maybe it's not about the happy ending. Maybe it's about the story.

—Unknown

You know what's always been a head-scratcher for me? Navigating the wild world of dating, love, attraction, and relationships. It's like a never-ending roller coaster of self-discovery, with each twist and turn teaching me something new about myself, others, and the crazy world we live in. And let me tell you, this ride ain't stopping anytime soon. It's a lifelong learning adventure, and I'm here for it!

As a child, my exposure to Disney fairy tales like *Sleeping Beauty*, *Snow White*, *Cinderella*, and *Beauty and the Beast* shaped my early perceptions of love and relationships. Our VHS machine played these movies on repeat. As a kid, I couldn't get enough of the princess being rescued by her knight in shining armor. I know I'm not alone! At a very young and impressionable age, these movies teach us an idealistic notion of love. The idea of being rescued from life's demons, effortlessly falling in love with a perfect prince, and living happily ever after (without much wisdom, experience, or effort) sounds incredible and too good to be true. And you know what? It is!

Throughout the ages, these fairy tales have endured the test of time, evolving through oral tradition with countless interpretations and retellings. The tale of *Sleeping Beauty*, for example, can be linked to the Italian story "Sun, Moon, and Talia" by Giambattista Basile, dating back to 1634. Similarly, *Snow White*'s roots can be found in German folklore, and the story eventually gained widespread fame through the Brothers Grimm rendition in 1812. Our perceptions of love and relationships are still influenced by these stories from the past.

In their book *Marriage and the Family in the Middle Ages*, Frances Gies and Joseph Gies discuss that the age at which men and women got married in the Middle Ages varied depending on factors such as social class, economic circumstances, and cultural norms. Noble and aristocratic individuals often married at a younger age, typically in their late teens or early twenties, for reasons such as political alliances and inheritance. Commoners, on the other hand, tended to marry later in life, often in their mid to late twenties, due to economic constraints and the need to establish themselves economically before starting a family. Arranged marriages were common across all social classes, and parental consent played a significant role in the marriage process, a practice that now seems outdated in modern times. During this period, women often had to rely on being "rescued" (i.e., married) by a metaphorical knight in shining armor to avoid becoming a spinster, as their financial stability was tied to these unions.[56] The shift from arranged marriages to relationships based on "love" is a complex process that has evolved over centuries. In Western societies, the rise of individualism and romantic ideals during the eighteenth and nineteenth centuries played a significant role in changing attitudes toward marriage. The Industrial Revolution and economic changes also provided individuals with more autonomy and freedom in choosing their partners. Then, the women's rights movement and changing gender roles in the twentieth century further contributed to the shift toward relationships based on "love" and mutual consent.

The marriages formed between two people in "love" might now be viewed as "puppy love" or "limerence." *Limerence*, a term coined by relationship expert Dorothy Tennov, is a psychological phenomenon rooted in romantic feelings toward another individual. It often manifests as intrusive thoughts, melancholic feelings, and worries about the object of affection. Those experiencing limerence often yearn for a deep emotional connection and the reciprocation of their feelings, sometimes to the point of obsession. This intense feeling of infatuation, excitement, butterflies, and a strong desire to be with a person feels amazing, but it can be blinding and not rooted in reality. It's idealistic, focusing on attraction and a naive belief in the perfection of the person and the relationship. Puppy love is just one stage of romantic relationships.

I recently had a puppy love story with someone, and it was a blast! However, I knew it was more of a short-term fling rather than a lifelong partnership. We had very different lives and saw the world very differently. We had a beautiful connection, though, that gave me the affection and attention I was craving at that time. That's the beauty of experience and wisdom kicking in, showing me that relationships come in all shapes and sizes. This awareness arrives with experience. Relationships can serve different purposes in our lives.

The issue with these fairy-tale scenarios lies in their reinforcement of outdated and false beliefs, setting unrealistic expectations that often lead to confusion and disappointment. Society's views on love and relationships have evolved significantly from the days of knights in shining armor and damsels in distress, but there is still some deprogramming to be done. I'd be dishonest if I claimed that I never daydream about being rescued by my own perfect prince during moments of anxiety, loneliness, or worry about my future and well-being. The notion of "being saved" is deeply ingrained in our minds, making it challenging to resist. But if you've ever been in a situation where you tried to save your partner or expected them to save you, you understand that ultimately, we can only save ourselves. Like Barry Manilow wrote in his book *Sweet Life*, "I believe that *we are who we choose to be*. Nobody is going to come and save you. You've got to save yourself. Nobody is going to give you anything. You've got to go out and fight for it."[57]

Also, in today's world, where people live nearly twice as long as when the traditional wedding vows were established, the notion of "till death do us part" may seem a bit unrealistic. This is not to say that a lifelong connection in which both parties evolve together is impossible—it certainly is! Anything is possible. However, the likelihood has shifted as we live longer and grow in unforeseeable directions, making it challenging to make such a definitive promise. This shift is reflected in the high divorce rates in the United States.[58] Additionally, with women now able to be financially independent and not rely on marriage for financial survival, the dynamics of relationships and commitments have further evolved.

I want to emphasize that it's not my place to dictate what type of relationship is suitable for anyone. We all have unique backgrounds, struggles, and desires. I don't claim to have all the answers, but through my dating experiences and keen observations, I've learned a few things. As we delve into the complex realm of romantic connections, my aim is to offer insights into fostering genuine, meaningful, and heartwarming connections. We will uncover the essence of love and understand what it means to both give and receive love in a world that is ever evolving.

LET'S TALK ABOUT ATTRACTION

You know, figuring out who I'm drawn to and why I've allowed certain individuals into my life was completely mind-boggling to me. I mean, I couldn't wrap my head around why I kept getting entangled with guys who just couldn't seem to show me genuine care. It got to the point where my own attraction patterns started to spook me a bit. Turns out, we often gravitate toward what feels familiar to us. It's like a subconscious pull toward what we've experienced before, even if it's not good for us. For instance, if you grew up in an environment where you faced neglect, you might unknowingly find yourself in a neglectful romantic relationship because that's what feels familiar and "normal" to you. A Heathline article titled "How to Recognize and Break Traumatic Bonds" states, "People who haven't experienced abuse often find it difficult to understand why people remain in abusive relationships. They might believe you're perfectly capable of leaving. In reality, though, the trauma bond makes this extremely difficult."[59]

And here's the thing: If we haven't taken the time to recognize our patterns and how we bond through trauma, we might find ourselves repeating the same unhealthy cycles with different partners. Now, when someone feels strangely familiar to me, instead of immediately jumping to the idea of soulmates from past lives (which, let's admit, is quite romantic), I pause and reflect on why their energy resonates with me and whether it's a positive influence in my life.

In my late twenties, I crossed paths with an Italian businessman. That feeling of familiarity struck a chord, considering my Italian roots and past attractions to Italian men. Despite his less-than-stellar looks and lack of personality, which had my friends scratching their heads, there was an intense magnetic pull between us. I could see the red flags early on, though: his controlling nature, his manipulative tendencies, and my suspicions of his fidelity. But the allure of our intense connection and the euphoric lovemaking kept me hooked.

During our intimate moments, I felt a mix of pain and love in my chest, a paradoxical sensation that left me spellbound. It was like a scene from a classic musical, with Frank Sinatra crooning in the background, "Bewitched (Bothered and Bewildered)." Seeking guidance, I returned to my weekly meditation group in Santa Monica and approached the instructor—he had a striking resemblance to a Hells Angels member, with his leather motorcycle jacket, tattoos, bald head, and a long white Santa Claus beard. I poured out my heart to him, confessing my infatuation with a guy who was clearly not the right fit for me, despite the intense connection we shared. Through tears, I explained that I had parted ways with the Italian businessman. With eagerness and vulnerability, I asked, "Is it possible to find that intense connection with someone who is a healthier match for me?"

In response, the instructor shared words that struck a chord deep within me. He gently remarked, "Probably not. You'll have to learn to love something different." Those words lingered in my mind, leaving a lasting impact on my path toward self-discovery and a healthier approach to love.

I had to choose myself over the addictive cycle of toxic passion. Despite the allure of those intense emotions, I knew I had grown too much to let a narcissist derail my progress. So, I made the courageous choice to prioritize my own well-being and figure out why I kept bringing the same type of man into my life.

I took a step back and really delved into why I was drawn to these men, what felt so familiar about them, and why they kept reappearing in my life. It struck me that these relationships were like a mirror reflecting the void within me, highlighting how I overlooked my own needs. The critical self-talk, tendency toward people-pleasing, struggle with setting boundaries, codependency, yearning for emotional validation, and low self-esteem echoed themes from my childhood, and it was all too familiar. I realized that what I was seeking from them—attention and love—was something I needed to give myself. They could never fill that void. Instead of constantly seeking external validation, I made a conscious decision to turn inward. I gave myself the attention and love I craved, nurturing myself from within. I began to see myself through the lens of my younger self, acknowledging her needs and desires. I started a heartfelt conversation with my inner child, providing the love and attention she longed for.

By nurturing and comforting little Giovanna, I redirected my energy toward self-healing and exited the loop of self-destruction. When I found myself in a place where I could confidently navigate dating again, if I went out with a man and recognized the familiar traits of a narcissistic pattern I had encountered before, I reminded myself not to fall back into that cycle. This required clear boundaries and a conscious decision to avoid diving into a relationship I knew would only lead to pain.

I wondered, though, if I would always be attracted to this type of person, and honestly, it felt like a curse. But then, the momentous *leap* occurred! It was another sunny day in Ubud, Bali, when I found myself on a lunch date with a guy I had connected with online. As we conversed, I couldn't ignore the familiar red flags and love-bombing tactics that had haunted me in the past, despite his charm and tall, tan, good looks. I sat there, engaged in the conversation, and couldn't help but chuckle to myself. Surprisingly, I felt no attraction toward him—on the contrary, I felt a sense of detachment. The fear of being drawn to him and the need to protect myself by running away had dissipated. I was finally learning to love something different.

#1 ATTRACTION ARSENAL

I've discovered that attraction is a major player in unconscious behavior. Even for the most emotionally intelligent people in the world, you can be having the time of your life on one side and feel like you've hit rock bottom on the flip side. To decode attraction in relationships, you have to step back and see the bigger picture.

Attraction can be a sign that we're seeking something in someone else that we are not aware of. Most of the time I find that it's not about the other person, but about fulfilling our own desires. It becomes a personal quest for what we crave and don't yet have. The key here is to recognize what you are wanting from that person. If we dig deep and are honest with ourselves about what we desire, we can bring the unconscious into conscious choice. To avoid falling into the attraction trap, ask yourself these questions:

- Why am I head over heels for this person?
- What feels oddly familiar in this attraction?
- What am I really after here?
- Is this the way to get what I truly desire?

Do a reality check and assess if jumping into a relationship aligns with your deepest desires and well-being. Keep in mind that initial attraction isn't synonymous with love; it can evolve into love over time, but at the start, it's driven by your unconscious desires. This is your cue to play detective and untangle the enigma of your heart's longings. So, take the reins and explore what it is you are genuinely looking for.

#2 ATTRACTION ARSENAL

Are we playing make-believe with our hearts? Guilty as charged! When we encounter someone who captivates us, it's easy to cast them as the protagonist in our personal fairy tale, fulfilling the role of "the one." In our meticulously crafted narrative, we paint an idealized picture of our perfect partner, blurring the boundaries between reality and fantasy. But here's the plot twist: Often we're not truly in love with the individual; we're infatuated with the character we've scripted for them. When they play their part according to our expectations, we admire them. However, the moment they step out of character, we disapprove. Our infatuation with the persona we've constructed blinds us to the real person standing in front of us.

It's a classic tale of self-deception—projecting our desires onto others and failing to see them for who they truly are. This sets an unfair standard for them and undermines the potential for a genuine connection. We also put ourselves in danger. If we project our fantasy on someone and they play along, what could they be hiding? By projecting our fantasies onto our romantic interests, we're not merely lost in a daydream—we're also assigning unhealthy meanings to our attraction. Let's keep these truths in mind:

- Feeling drawn to someone doesn't automatically mean they're "the one."
- Attraction doesn't necessarily signify a predestined partnership.
- A spark of interest isn't a cosmic sign guiding us to our perfect match. It might just be a cosmic sign guiding us back to ourselves.
- Being attracted to someone doesn't guarantee compatibility or a future together.

It's time to step out of the fairy tale and into reality, where genuine connections are built on mutual understanding, acceptance, and authenticity. I'll admit, I still find myself slipping into fairy-tale mode when I meet someone special. But I've learned to catch myself in the act and snap back to the present moment. The real deal is far more interesting. Engaging fully with someone and truly seeing them for who they are is so much more fulfilling than getting lost in a world of illusions. Instead of trying to change someone into our perfect image, let's focus on valuing them for their one-of-a-kind essence. Isn't that what we all want? To be seen and loved for who we are, without the need for masks and pretenses?

It's time to rewrite the script and open ourselves up to the complexities of real relationships, free from the illusions of our fantasies.

#3 ATTRACTION ARSENAL

One of the ways I shielded myself from falling back into a toxic relationship was by recognizing what I sought from a partner and learning to fulfill those needs within myself. A practice that helped me was connecting with my inner child and addressing her unmet needs. Renowned psychotherapist Joan E. Childs sheds light on the significance of inner child work, emphasizing how unresolved childhood wounds manifest in our relationships unconsciously:

As the years passed, the need for Inner Child Work grew. . . . We now know that what was once thought of as "fringe" or "pop psychology" has become a well-accepted modality for not just the recovering population, but anyone who has been abused, abandoned, and neglected in their childhood. The wounds of the child remain in our psyche and get acted out in our relationships unconsciously. We unconsciously choose a partner that will give us the worst nightmare in order to resolve our unresolved childhood wounds. Then we fire them for the very reason we hired them. It is impossible to have relational maturity until we cleanse our childhood traumas. Most of us did not have a secure relationship as children so we spend the rest of our lives looking for the love that was denied us in all the wrong places. . . . The only way out is through! The pain of healing is nothing compared to the pain of suffering unresolved trauma.[60]

To start the healing process with my inner child, I wrote her a letter. I validated little Giovanna's emotions and struggles, reassuring her that she bears no guilt or shame. I emphasized that her feelings are valid, pain is a natural part of the human experience, and it's okay to not be okay. I asked her what she needed and how I could help her. The letter ended with me telling her she is accepted and eternally loved. If this hits home, I encourage you to write your own letter to little you. You never know what wisdom she might share!

IT'S NOT PERSONAL

In Tenerife, Spain, on one of my solo-traveling adventures, I crossed paths with this Italian guy who caught my eye . . . I know, shocker, right? We'll call him Fabio.

So, Fabio invited me to dinner, and despite enjoying his company, it became pretty clear off the bat that his attention span was about as fleeting as a shooting star. He interrupted me midsentence, struggled to hold eye contact, and scanned the room like he was on some undercover CIA mission waiting for the prime suspect to stroll in. He mentioned hitting up a beach club the next day at 4 p.m., and since I was keen on checking out that spot and we did have a decent time together despite his attention quirks, I agreed. Fast-forward to the next morning, when I excitedly went shopping for a beach cover, got my nails done, and kept it light on the food to rock my bikini. I was looking forward to it, you know?

As the clock inched closer to 4 p.m., there was radio silence. I gave it until 5 p.m., thinking he'd surely reach out. But nope, nada, no text, no call from him. So, I texted, "Hey, are we still on for the beach club?" And his reply? "Hey, how's it going? Yeah, we should totally hit the beach club, but I need to sort out some house stuff. How about we meet up later instead, say 8:30 p.m.?" Annoyed and puzzled by why he hadn't told me this earlier, I agreed to meet later.

Come 8:30 p.m.—crickets. No word from Mr. Fabio. I didn't hear from him until the next afternoon: "I messed up, I'm really sorry for wasting your time. I struggle with focusing and when I have a lot on my plate, I lose interest in everything. I pondered all day on what to say, and I want to be honest with you. I would really like to see you again though."

Now, the old me would've taken him ghosting me personally and spiraled into self-doubt and blame. *He's not interested because I'm not captivating enough, not attractive enough, too assertive . . .* you name it. I would have dwelled in a pit of despair, fuming over how he made me feel, and probably would have written a scathing response.

But this current version of me? I didn't let it shake my confidence. I realized it wasn't about me; it was his deal, not mine. People are who they are, and I don't have to turn everything into a personal drama. So, instead of wallowing and retaliating, I replied, "Thanks for being up front but I don't think we are a good match. I hope you find the support you need. Take care." It felt empowering not to internalize it. I maintained my grace even when ghosted, showing up as my best self and not the insecure scorned girl from my past. Maybe we could've had a blast at the beach club, but he was stuck in his ways. I'm not about to push something that isn't flowing naturally. Forcing things usually spells trouble. If the universe is nudging you in a direction, it's best to go with the flow. Whenever I've tried to push things, it usually backfires. Let things come and go, including people. Letting go can be tough, but it's a skill worth mastering.

This is just one of the many stories I have about men who seemed interested but couldn't quite get out of their own way. You know the clichés like, "If he really wanted to, he would," or "He's just not that into you"? People like to throw these out as blanket "truth-telling" statements in all dating disappointments, but this isn't necessarily the case in every situation, and even if it were, the reality is not as personal as those statements sound. It's unfair to assume that every man is a confident, bold knight in shining armor (here's the fairy-tale projection again) ready to go after everything he wants. Personally, I tend to be drawn to more reserved guys because I'm outgoing. These timid types aren't smooth, suave Don Juan characters who fake it till they make it. Sometimes, someone might not pursue you because they're afraid of letting you down, not in the right headspace, or just plain scared. It could be overwhelming for them. We all have our struggles, and sometimes we don't know what others are dealing with.

When "he's just not that into you" applies, and we have all been there, remember that someone not being interested in you is not a reflection of your worth. People have different preferences, attractions (as discussed earlier—we know how complicated the attraction game can be), and reasons for not pursuing a romantic connection. In no way does this mean there is something wrong with you. At the end of the day, if they're not into it for whatever reason, just take it in stride and keep moving forward with your chin up. I'm all about respecting people's boundaries and decisions. It reminds me of this sweet eighty-eight-year-old lady I met on a train once, who told me, "Don't worry if it doesn't work out with a man. There are plenty of other moms with nice sons."

One big reason we often take things personally is because we automatically think someone's actions or words are all about us. This is when we need to remind ourselves that everyone has insecurities, fears, and emotions that shape how they act or speak. We give people power over our emotions when we internalize their words and actions. Here's a scenario: Say your partner's having a rough day and snaps at you. Instead of jumping to the conclusion that you messed up somehow, think about the possibility that they're just stressed about work or other stuff going on. By pausing and not instantly making it all about you, you can handle the situation with grace and understanding. Choosing not to take things personally allows us to maintain inner peace.

We all see the world through our unique lens of experiences and emotions. Writer Jennifer Livingstone summarizes the wisdom of Don Miguel Ruiz in a post about *The Four Agreements*: "Nothing others do is because of you. What others say and do is a projection of their own reality, their own dream. When you are immune to the opinions and actions of others, you won't be the victim of needless suffering."[61] I may not be

100 percent there yet, but I'm on the path to freedom from seeking validation from others, and my self-worth has never been stronger. Like a butterfly gliding past, let's not let the opinions and actions of others weigh us down.

EXPECTATIONS VERSUS STANDARDS

Let me start by breaking down the concepts of expectations and standards. According to the good ol' *Oxford English Dictionary*, the definition of *expectation* is "the action or fact of anticipating or foreseeing something; the belief that something will happen or be the case."[62] The *Merriam-Webster Dictionary* defines *standard* as "something established by authority, custom, or general consent as a model or example."[63] It can also refer to a set of rules or principles that are widely recognized and followed. Navigating the dating scene has taught me a valuable lesson in distinguishing between expectations and standards, guiding me toward a more peaceful way of being. I've come to realize that expectations, often driven by unrealistic ideals, can pave the way for disappointment.

Navigating expectations can be tricky because what seems like a simple and normal request to us may be entirely unrealistic for someone else. My friend Anna has become a pro at managing expectations within her marriage. Anna has a passion for exquisite jewelry, and for years, she expected her husband to surprise her with luxurious pieces. However, she soon realized that this expectation was unrealistic for him. He doesn't have a clue about jewelry. Instead of continually feeling let down by the gifts she received and him feeling pressured, Anna came up with a clever solution. She set up a bank account where her husband deposits money as a gift. Then she treats herself to the jewelry she adores. I thought this was a brilliant idea, and it's a win-win for everyone involved!

On the flip side, standards are the cornerstone of my dating philosophy, grounded in my values and principles. It's essential that those who share their time with me honor their commitments and, if circumstances prevent them from doing so, communicate openly and honestly. Reflecting on the past encounter with Fabio, I learned that expecting him to follow through on his promises was not only normal but also a reflection of my own standards. However, I also understood that his inability to do so stemmed from his own issues, making it an unrealistic expectation.

You know, keeping my word is a big deal for me—it's a standard I hold highly. If I commit to something, I follow through. And if things change, I try to give a heads-up early on. The thought of leaving someone hanging or undervalued really hits home for me; I just can't bring myself to do that. When others flake on me, it leaves me feeling all kinds of frustrated and disappointed. But here's the thing: I reached a point where I was fed up with feeling this way. I realized that holding on to that frustration only hurt me because the other person might not even care. So, how did I find peace with this?

I discovered that life feels much lighter and more joyful when I stopped expecting and started accepting. I had to come to terms with the fact that not everyone will show up as promised, literally or figuratively. But this doesn't mean I have to lower my standards. While I choose to let go of those who don't match their words with actions, I've learned not to be attached to expectations. My fellow Confused Girl, it's time to take a step back and reflect on your expectations in dating and relationships. Are they constantly setting you up for disappointment? Consider shifting from expectations to acceptance—it's a game changer that can bring you peace.

Take a moment to jot down your relationship standards. These are the nonnegotiables that define how you want to be treated and set the boundaries for your happiness. For instance, valuing emotional availability and effective communication can steer you away from settling for a partner who isn't fully invested in the relationship. And listen, I understand how difficult this can be if you are in love with someone. I have been blinded by love, infatuation, and lust more times than I can count. However, holding on to unrealistic expectations that someone who is emotionally distant will suddenly become emotionally available can lead to a cycle of frustration and pain. By knowing and living by your personal standards, you empower yourself to avoid settling for anything less than you deserve. With grace and self-respect, you can confidently say, *NEXT!* and move forward without feeling disappointed or undervalued.

And if you're in a happy, committed marriage or relationship where you find yourself expecting something from your partner that they aren't able to give, it might be time to shift gears. Try trading expectations for acceptance and find a solution like my friend Anna did. By seeking a solution that satisfies both of you, you create harmony within your relationship.

So, my dear friend, I think you can now see how understanding our attraction to others is like holding up a mirror to ourselves. It's a powerful tool that can help us uncover the parts of ourselves that need attention and care. Instead of falling into the same old patterns with different people, we can take a beat and consciously decide what we truly want in our lives.

Understanding our attraction, not taking things personally, and distinguishing between expectations and standards can transform the way we approach dating and relationships. We can bring peace to an area of our lives that once felt chaotic and painful. It's about growth, self-discovery, and building deeper connections with others. Remember, you've got this! I believe in you.

CONFUSED GIRL RECAP:

- Unravel the attraction mystery by acknowledging that attraction reflects hidden desires and unmet needs within you. By taking a step back and examining the bigger picture, we can decode the messages our attractions are sending us. To break free from unconscious attraction patterns, ask yourself these questions: Why are you drawn to a particular person? What familiar feelings arise in this attraction? What deep desires are you seeking to fulfill? Is this attraction aligned with your true desires and well-being?

- Real connections are grounded in mutual respect and authenticity, not idealized fairy tales. When we project fantasies onto others, we create unrealistic expectations that hinder genuine understanding and acceptance. By seeing individuals for who they truly are, beyond the roles we assign them, we create deeper connections based on appreciation and acceptance.

- Your inner child holds the key to your relationship patterns. Try connecting with your inner child and acknowledge their past pain and struggles. Writing a letter to your inner child can be a powerful tool in validating emotions and addressing unmet needs.

- Understanding that people's behaviors and words are shaped by their own insecurities, fears, and emotions is essential in avoiding unnecessary suffering and conflict. It's easy to take things personally and assume that someone else's actions are all about us, but everyone has their own struggles and experiences that influence how they interact with others.

- Expectations are uncertain beliefs about future outcomes that can end in disappointment if our desired outcome is not met. Standards reflect personal values and set boundaries for self-respect and integrity. The ability to shift from expectations to acceptance can bring peace and empowerment in relationships. But holding clear standards for yourself ensures that you don't settle for less than you deserve.

CHAPTER 10

Be Unstoppable

If you realized how beautiful you are, you'd fall at your own feet.

—Byron Katie

This may sound overly dramatic, but there was a time in my life when I had to face a gale-force wind of catastrophe. When that storm hit and brought me to my knees, I didn't hide. I surrendered. I built a humbler, stronger, and wiser self. I didn't run and I didn't break. I bent into something more beautiful. I became stronger. I decided that I was worth investing in, took the steps to build a better me and a more genuine self—a me that was doing things from my soul, not just the default ego. I soaked up wisdom like a sponge, put it into action, and believed that life could feel better and be better than what I was experiencing. That's why in the core of my being, this Confused Girl knows she's unstoppable. And I know something else: You're unstoppable too.

I learned this life-affirming lesson by believing and working toward my dreams. In those moments of transformation, I discovered the power of resilience and the beauty of authenticity. It wasn't about changing who I was; it was about becoming who I was meant to be. Each challenge faced and each lesson learned were stepping stones guiding me toward a life that resonated with my true nature. The journey wasn't easy, but it was undeniably worth it. And as I continue to grow and evolve, I carry with me the unwavering belief that we all have an inner strength capable of overcoming any adversity.

When I started my blog and activewear line, I was only just beginning to walk my path of transformation. Returning to LA after working at the restaurant felt like a time warp. My lifeline at the time was my new company. It was entirely my own, something I knew I could grow into. I threw myself into the work, knowing it was for the business, but also for me. For several years, my days and nights revolved around building this project. I created my activewear before everyone and their mother were designing yoga pants. When I came on the scene, yoga apparel was basically an itty-bitty business; there were only Lululemon and a few other yoga wear lines—and me. But within this small world, I was convinced I had the most gorgeous and wholly original concept: crystal-inspired designer leggings.

Almost every waking hour, I dedicated myself to growing my Confused Girl in the City brand. Every cent I earned from part-time jobs went back into the company. I spent months searching for the right manufacturer, and then it took another four months of testing samples to get them just right. Once I had my creations in hand, I blasted hundreds of emails to showrooms. As I mentioned earlier, it was a huge feat to have my leggings accepted into the downtown LA New Mart Building. But I didn't stop there. I also went door-to-door speaking with shop owners, trying to convince them to carry my products, and spent countless hours vending at fairs and markets. I sent out press releases to hundreds of publications. At the same time, I stayed laser-focused on growing my Instagram account so I could spread my message. Let me give a shout-out right now to my terrific team of interns who helped me spread the word—thank you!

Following three years of intense, breathless, relentless, and persistent hustle, I was selling thousands of my products all over the world—from California to South Korea. When one of my former interns emailed and wrote that she'd seen a girl in Munich, Germany, biking past her wearing my Simplicity Leggings, I was blown away. It meant a lot to me, not just because my leggings were selling, but because I see Confused Girl as more than just a clothing line; I see it as a movement for *us*. It's a way for modern women warriors to find and honor their true, powerful, unstoppable natures. Knowing that girls from all over the world were now part of this movement inspired me to continue giving my absolute all. Everything I had.

If I needed any more encouragement, I got it. A few weeks later, I was scouting for a photo shoot on Venice Beach when a young woman walked up to me and asked if I was the Confused Girl from Instagram. "That's me!" I said, holding myself back from hugging her. Then she told me she had bought my Sincere Leggings. The rest of the day I was floating.

Did I say dreams come true?

If that wasn't enough wish fulfillment, my line was featured on the cover of *LA Yoga*. After writing almost every month to the publisher, I got a surprise email from the editor. They had a photo shoot coming up and needed leggings. Faster than the speed of light, I packed a suitcase filled to the top with my line and drove like a maniac to their office, schlepping every single leggings option I had. Six weeks later, my leggings were on the cover. I saw that magazine in doctor's offices, health food stores, gyms, and fitness studios all over the city. What a thrill! To show my appreciation, I sent a magnificent bouquet of flowers to the editor along with a note expressing my sincere thanks.

Even though I was a wildly busy Confused Girl, over those years I learned a lot about how to take care of myself: keep things in perspective, honor the path I am traveling, and feel grateful for the way life is unfolding.

Then, the detour happened.

THE HIDDEN GIFT

As I've learned, nothing stays the same—and that includes success, especially when it comes to sales. I was in Bali, where I chose to work on my book in peaceful surroundings while managing the business from afar. But something was happening back home, and it wasn't good news, or so I originally believed. I got word that my sales were dramatically dropping.

Six years after starting my company, more competition had entered the market, and other yoga-wear companies were targeting my customers. Their items were a lot less expensive than mine. While I was manufacturing exquisite products in the US and Europe, some of my competitors were opting to make lesser-quality goods in China. Even though their products couldn't compare with my line, their stuff was a lot cheaper. "I'll never be able to compete" was my first reaction.

But hold on! Over the years, I had gone through so many struggles, worked so hard on myself to grow and commit to a deeper and more authentic path, and I wasn't going to let this setback destroy me. Instead, this Confused Girl vowed to open herself up to new possibilities—and to trust. First, to settle my sizzling anxiety, I used the deep breathing method I had learned in the Santa Monica meditation sessions. Then I sat under one of Bali's banyan trees—the same kind of tree the Buddha sat under when he became enlightened. I'm no Buddha and I didn't get enlightened, but I know how to ask questions, and my mind was churning: *Where is the world trying to guide me? How can this turn into a positive situation in my life? What other possibilities can I explore at this time? How can I use everything I've learned and turn this into something that will lead to the next great adventure?*

After Bali, I continued my travels in writing this book and lived in Greece and Thailand, visited Spain, Italy, Austria, Singapore, Malaysia, and Switzerland, and returned to Bali before settling in Germany. This entire book was written while I traveled the world, learning and experiencing many valuable lessons.

The slowdown of my business was actually a gift.

If my company had continued to expand, I would have been forced to return home and oversee the business through this new competitive market. Writing this book may have needed to take a back seat. Instead, I realized that though sales were slowing down, the business remained manageable from abroad, which was exactly what I needed. I was so grateful that my business had boomed when it did; otherwise I wouldn't have had the money to travel abroad and write this book.

I bow down to the timing of the universe. It knows what it's doing.

STEPPING INTO A NEW ROLE

No longer able to completely rely on my clothing sales for financial support, I was lucky to fall into becoming an influencer while promoting my activewear on Instagram. It was a win-win. The campaigns and collaborations I've since done with different brands have brought me not only joy but increasing recognition.

Among the many collaborations, one of my favorites was the Audi campaign in Germany. Embarking on an unforgettable road trip with my close friend in the passenger seat, I drove a stunning Audi Q3 through Bavaria, Austria, and then the Italian Dolomites. It was the end of March, and snow was still on the mountains. The views were breathtaking. At first, our soundtrack was our own *oohs* and *aahs*, but then as the scenery started looking like the movie version of *The Chronicles of Narnia*, we began belting out Alanis Morissette's "Wunderkind"—a tune from the film's soundtrack. It's a memory forever etched in my mind.

What made this collaboration even more remarkable? I was one of the very first female influencers to partner with Audi Deutschland, a predominantly male-run company. I feel overwhelmingly appreciative that I was given the opportunity to pave the way for more female influencers to enter this market. Breakthroughs all around. *Danke!*

FEEL YOUR FEELINGS

All this said, I didn't instantly feel upbeat and empowered when

I got the bad sales news, and great things didn't happen to me overnight. There were a few grim weeks when I asked the right questions, but the answers were filled with self-pity and self-recrimination. I gave myself time to wallow and made space for some serious sobbing. I let my mind blame myself for the company's losses. I overate and overslept. But after three weeks of wallowing, I shook myself out of it. Because of the work I had done on myself over the previous years and the lessons I had learned, I could move on. I was refreshed and ready to run.

What I want you to know, Confused Sisters, is that this curve in the road and the necessary change in direction didn't happen overnight, and it wasn't an immediate smooth, happy-go-lucky transition. When things don't go the way we want, we often need to go through a mourning process. Please, don't push it away. I definitely experienced this period of sadness and disappointment. But unlike the old Giovanna, I didn't get stuck in the quicksand of feeling bad. I didn't hang out there for too long, and I wouldn't let it take me over. If I had allowed myself to dwell in the landscape of "should've, would've, could've," I might have missed the bigger picture—the one pointing the way to a solution.

I'm in total agreement with author and Buddhist meditation teacher Sharon Salzberg, who wrote in her book *Real Love: The Art of Mindful Connection*, "When we learn to respond to disappointments with acceptance, we give ourselves the space to realize that all our experiences—good and bad alike—are opportunities to learn and grow."[64] If I were still bemoaning the loss of sales and ruminating over things that appeared to go wrong, I would probably also be locked in a depression right now. But on the contrary, I'm filled with appreciation for the success the brand has brought me and the experiences I've had.

KEYS TO BOUNCING BACK

These are several techniques I use to lift my spirit. They may work for you; they may not. But if you're dealing with disappointment—whether it's a love affair gone sour, a business gone bust, or a friendship in the dumps—you probably don't have much to lose by trying a few of these suggestions. Start with the keys that resonate within you.

KEY ONE: LET IT OUT

Forget the stiff-upper-lip bit. It feels good to release our emotions. This might mean a good cry-your-eyes-out or a scream-at-the-top-of-your-lungs. In the process you'll reduce your stress and may get over your disappointment sooner. According to Stephen Sideroff, a clinical psychologist at UCLA, "Crying activates the body in a healthy way. . . . Letting down one's guard and one's defenses and [crying] is a very positive, healthy thing. The same thing happens when you watch a movie and it touches you and you cry . . . That process of opening into yourself . . . it's like a lock and key."[65]

KEY TWO: TAKE CARE OF YOUR BODY

It's not easy to be emotionally down and still take care of yourself, but it's the best thing you can do. Instead of eating poorly, drinking too much, or smoking weed, choose healthy options on menus or at the grocery store. Try at least one week of sobriety and see how it feels both mentally and physically. Combine this with some form of daily body movement, even if it's simply a twenty-minute walk. We need to think clearly in order to understand that there is a positive side—and a way out. Keeping your body open is a great support to that process.

KEY THREE: SURROUND YOURSELF WITH SUPPORT

When in crisis, don't hesitate to reach out for professional support, whether a therapist or a counselor. This should be your first step. If you have a really good friend, someone you've known for some time and who has proven herself to be trusting, compassionate, and supportive, you can also lean on her. Talking through your ideas and expressing your feelings with someone you trust can make a world of difference. It's important to have that outlet during tough times. Personally, I don't know what I would do without my handful of best girlfriends. They are my personal support system, and I'm theirs. We help each other figure things out by talking it through.

KEY FOUR: VIEW YOUR PAST DISAPPOINTMENT AS A LEARNING EXPERIENCE

It may sound like a cliché to say, "Life is always giving us lessons," but, girl, I testify that it's 100 percent true. Don't be hard on yourself; it's part of the process. When something disappointing has happened, meditate on what you can learn from it. Keep returning to meditation since the lesson might not arrive right away. Give yourself time. Understand that personal growth often requires patience and persistence. When you're ready—move on. Remember, every setback is a setup for a comeback, so trust in the journey and continue to evolve.

KEY FIVE: ASK YOURSELF WHAT THE UNIVERSE/GOD (WHATEVER YOU WANT TO CALL IT) IS TRYING TO TELL YOU

I find it helpful to be introspective and seek meaning behind the challenges I'm facing in the present moment. I might ask myself, *Do I need to slow down? Am I taking the wrong turn? Is there something else waiting in the wings that I'm not seeing? Have I forgotten the power of gratitude?* I've found that connecting with a sense of purpose or a higher power comforts and strengthens me during adversity. It also gives me answers.

KEY SIX: RECONNECT WITH YOURSELF

When I've fallen into a rut, it's usually because I've been running on autopilot. Hey, it happens. We're busy. We have to get a lot of stuff done, and it feels like there's no time to stop and ask ourselves, *What's going on with me?* But inevitably when I'm going through a long period like that, I eventually crash. When that happens, I don't try to fight it. I go with it. I stop. I quiet down. I give myself at least one day to do nothing but relax. I might unplug to recharge. I might get a massage or take a luxurious bath. This is a personal choice. Ask yourself: *What nourishes me?*

KEY SEVEN: USE WHAT'S IN YOUR TOOLBOX

I've shared dozens of strategies that have helped me on my path. Some of these strategies require practice. If they were easy, we probably would have been using them all along. But persistence and discipline pay off. If I didn't know from my experience that these tools work, I wouldn't have included them. I want every Confused Girl to grow into a free warrior. So, grab a tool and build a bold new life! If something doesn't help you, so what? Love yourself for trying and choose a different one.

KEY EIGHT: GET BACK IN THE GAME

So, even though my online shop doesn't financially support me anymore, I still find joy in selling my products to loyal customers and creating new ones. Seeing women wearing my designs on social media brings me so much happiness and fulfillment. It's not just about the money for me; it's about the passion and creativity that goes into each piece.

I could have easily given up and closed my shop, but I chose to keep going because of the joy it brings me. There is a time to count your losses and head out, but I never recommend it unless you're absolutely sure. It's not a decision that should be made hastily. My philosophy is to give whatever you're doing (as long as it's not self-destructive) at least one last chance but with a new lens of awareness—*what needs changing, if anything?*

It's up to you. Intuitively, you'll know what's best.

BUILDING SELF-CONFIDENCE

If you want to be unstoppable, you have to believe in yourself. That takes self-confidence. Most of us are born believing in ourselves, but somewhere along the way, especially for girls, we stop trusting our own view of the world. We second-guess our opinions. We think someone else knows better. We don't believe we have what it takes. Katty Kay and Claire Shipman, authors of the book *The Confidence Code for Girls*, along with the polling firm *Ypulse*, surveyed 1,300 girls between the ages of eight and eighteen and their parents. The authors found that "confidence levels are evenly matched for boys and girls until the age of 12. But between the ages of 8 and 14, girls' confidence levels nose-dive by 30 percent."[66]

You know what I say to that? Girls, you've got what it takes—and more. Let's not waste another one of our precious minutes believing we're less than. Let's boost our confidence right here and now. Here are my five favorite ways to do it:

1. *Keep learning.* When we gain knowledge about a subject, it automatically makes us feel better about ourselves. Take a course online or go to classes on a subject that interests you. We all feel more confident when we feel smart.

2. *Take a shot.* Don't let fear of failure or perfectionism paralyze you—and don't worry about the results of your attempt. Remember from chapter two, there's no such thing as failure! It's nothing more than a perspective, and perspectives can be turned around. Failure isn't a fixed truth; it's a belief that can change depending on how you see things. It's important to stay courageous. Focus on what's most important: Do the work and don't worry about the results.

3. *Don't allow yourself to be jealous of anyone's accomplishments.* When you're unstoppable, you nurture the mindset to want what's best for *everyone*, even your competitors. Why? Because their success doesn't mean that you won't make it. The small-mindedness of jealousy and envy is hung up in our ego, and it's an energy sucker. Stay in the confidence zone. Our unstoppable soul knows there's room for everyone to be happy. Now, that's an energizing thought!

4. *Begin now.* A lot of people wait to start working on their dream come true because they don't have enough money or time, or they don't believe they have the right connections to succeed. Being confident is a mindset based on your belief in yourself—not on your circumstances or the people around you. It also takes practice. The more you get up and do it,

the more equipped you become. Be unstoppable by working toward making your dream come true, even before you have everything set in place.

5. *Don't base your success on how much money you've made.* Of course, it's great to have nice things and cash in the bank—and we definitely don't want to live under the shadow of a mountain of debt. But we also don't want to measure our self-worth by how much money we have. Push your personal limits without considering external rewards. True success should be measured by the impact you have on others and the fulfillment you have with the life you've created. Success is not defined by the size of your wallet but by the depth of your character and the difference you make in the world.

IMPULSIVE VERSUS SPONTANEOUS

On our way to being unstoppable, lots of opportunities will present themselves. If you make a quick decision to grab that chance, make sure it's coming from a place of spontaneity, not impulsiveness. While these two actions are often mentioned in the same breath, they're not the same things. Impulsive actions are made with little thought or consideration of the consequences. I should know.

During the COVID-19 pandemic, I impulsively invested in five hundred Pilates rings from China with the intention of selling them on Amazon, only to realize that the low-quality rings were unsalable due to their poor construction. I lost $2,000 and had nowhere to store five hundred Pilates rings. The lesson from this experience is to exercise caution and do thorough research before making quick business decisions! Reflecting on this impulsive bulk purchase, I realized that my actions were driven by fear and anxiety. *I need to do something and make money during COVID.* I was also motivated by greed, thinking, *I've heard of many people making millions on Amazon with silly products.* Nothing about this venture felt exciting, inspired, or joyful. Germaine Greer, the kick-ass feminist, said, "The essence of pleasure is spontaneity."[67] True spontaneity should feel good, and your gut should tell you to go for it. With spontaneity, you make decisions from a big-picture perspective without getting hung up on expectations. You're ready to act—but not from a place of fear, anxiety, or greed.

If you feel confident and happy that your decision to move forward is right for everyone involved, trust it. Several months ago, I had the most enchanting dream about floating over a waterfall surrounded by breathtaking beauty. When I woke up, I couldn't get Iceland out of my mind. That afternoon I spontaneously booked a ticket. Because of my growing role as an influencer, I was able to get a bunch of collaborations with hotels, restaurants, and tour companies—and it helped propel me further as a solo female travel influencer.

My unforgettable month in Iceland was one of the most mystical experiences of my life. It nurtured my understanding that my only true purpose on Earth is to live authentically and grow. If you've worked toward your dream, feel good about trusting your intuition and instincts to move forward on something. Go ahead—be spontaneous.

ADMITTING MISTAKES

I still feel remorseful whenever I remember the year that I was so wrapped up in my own life, I unintentionally forgot my friend

Anna's birthday. Not surprisingly, she was hurt, disappointed, and deservedly a little pissed off. Anna is always on top of these kinds of things and has never missed a chance to celebrate my birthday—as well as my accomplishments. I mean, she's just the best friend any Confused Girl could hope to have. The next day when I realized my mistake, I was mortified. The last thing I ever wanted was to give Anna the impression that she isn't one of the most important people in my life.

I immediately reached out to her by phone and apologized profusely for missing her special day. Even though this was a time in my life when I was working on overdrive and trying to balance a million things at once, there was no excuse—and I made that clear to my dear friend. A few days later, I took her out for a special dinner at her favorite restaurant and gave her a gift certificate for a deluxe massage. Then I raised a glass of champagne to my bestie: "Anna, I vow to never forget another birthday—and may there be a gazillion more that we celebrate together!"

I stand by this law of the universe: *Do the right thing!* That definitely means taking responsibility for our mistakes. It's not easy, believe me, I know—but it's the only way to be respected and trusted. It's proof to others, and to ourselves, that we are accountable for our actions and we take responsibility for our lives.

If you've made a mistake that involved another person like I did with Anna's birthday, you can take these steps to accept responsibility—and then move on.

- Acknowledge the mistake.
- Sincerely apologize.
- Explain what happened (without making excuses).
- Remedy the situation.

Also, forgive yourself. Of course, it's a cliché to say "every-one makes mistakes"—but everyone *does*. So, don't let a faux pas stop you. Just tell it like it is. Research shows that leaders who admit their mistakes are viewed more positively; they are demonstrating a level of humility, which is an attractive and honorable trait.[68]

LAST WORDS

When I pulled myself out of despair several years ago, I built a stronger self that was based on everything I've shared with you. I did it so that I could navigate the ups and downs of my life in a healthier way. And there will always be ups and downs until the day we take our last breath. All we can do is learn how to deal with the ride in the most graceful, least self-sabotaging, least self-blaming way. That's what being unstoppable means. You deal—and you go on.

I encourage you, my fellow Confused Girl, to embrace brav-ery, patience, persistence, and self-confidence in your quest for self-discovery. Remember, within the depths of confusion lies the potential for something extraordinary to emerge. Even when you are faced with challenging lessons, something beautiful always awaits you. Allow yourself to unwrap the gift and explore.

Embrace confusion as a virtue, for I promise, it will guide you to uncover hidden truths and untapped potential. Confu-sion is a powerful teacher pushing us to grow and evolve. So, remain open and curious. Believe in your ability to perceive your life in a healthier and more empowered way. Know that you have the innate ability to liberate yourself from outdated thought patterns that no longer serve you, and grow into the bigger life that awaits you.

My friend, you possess the power to shape your own extraordinary existence. I implore you to go forth and fearlessly unleash the badass that is within you. Never forget . . .

YOU ARE UNSTOPPABLE!

CONFUSED GIRL RECAP:

- *Rely on these valuable keys to bouncing back:* Release your emotions—cry your eyes out or scream at the top of your lungs to reduce stress and get over disappointment. Take care of your body by choosing healthy options and give yourself a week of sobriety to think clearly. Surround yourself with support—call your best friend or seek advice from a counselor. View disappointment as a learning experience and meditate on what you can learn from it. Ask yourself what the universe is trying to tell you and connect with a sense of purpose. Reconnect with yourself by taking a day to relax and nourish yourself. Use the tools in this book to build a bold new life with a new lens of awareness.

- If you want to be unstoppable, you have to believe in yourself. That takes self-confidence. To build self-confidence, keep learning, take courageous action, avoid jealousy, start pursuing your dreams, and don't use money as the measure of your success. Prioritize growth and awareness. Taking steps toward goals without waiting for perfect conditions showcases determination and resilience. Embracing a mindset of abundance and supporting others' success without envy cultivates a strong sense of self-worth.

By embodying self-assurance and pursuing personal growth with determination, you can build a foundation of unwavering confidence in the face of challenges.

- When faced with opportunities, choose spontaneity over impulsiveness to make decisions from a place of composure and joy, focusing on the big picture without fear or greed. Trust your gut feelings and move forward confidently for the betterment of all involved. Also, don't be afraid to admit mistakes and take responsibility. Everyone makes mistakes, and humility is an attractive and honorable trait in leadership and personal relationships. Apologize sincerely, explain the situation without making excuses, and take steps to remedy the error. Forgiving oneself and moving forward with honesty and integrity demonstrates a commitment to doing the right thing.

- Confusion is a powerful teacher, guiding you to uncover hidden truths and untapped potential. Learn from challenges and remain open to growth and evolution. Believe in your ability to perceive life in a healthier and more empowered way, liberating yourself from outdated thought patterns. You possess the power to shape your extraordinary existence and unleash the badass within you. Be brave, patient, and persistent in your quest for self-discovery, knowing that within confusion lies the potential for something incredible to emerge.

Acknowledgments

I want to express my heartfelt gratitude to all the amazing Confused Girls who bravely chose to grab a copy of this book and embark on a journey to discover their true selves.

A special shout-out goes to my agent, Marilyn Allen, and my editor at Blackstone Publishing, Marilyn Kretzer, for their unwavering belief in the Confused Girl message. To everyone at Blackstone Publishing: Your incredible support has been a driving force.

I can't thank my dear friends Kat Waller and Christina Constabile enough for being my pillars of strength throughout this adventure. From diving into my chapters to late-night life talks, your constant encouragement lifted me up even in moments of doubt. You both are truly remarkable souls in my life.

My heartfelt appreciation goes out to my parents for their undying support and love. And I send a loving tribute to my father. Thank you for instilling in me the value of perseverance. Without that lesson, this book would not have come to fruition.

About the Author

Giovanna Silvestre, a graduate of the University of Southern California with a degree in international relations, initially found success in the entertainment industry. But after pulling back the veil and experiencing the darker sides of the business, she made the decision to leave behind its superficial glitz and glamour in search of self-discovery. This journey led her to become a popular influencer and the creator of Confused Girl in the City, an international activewear brand. Each design in her collection is inspired by a unique healing crystal, adding a touch of beauty and spirituality to her brand.

Giovanna has been featured on NBC and in publications such as *Forbes*, *Yoga Magazine*, and *LA Yoga*. In the process of writing *Confused Girl: Find Your Peace in the Chaos*, Giovanna embarked on a transformative adventure, living solo in various parts of the world, including Indonesia, Thailand, Italy, and Germany. These experiences, combined with the valuable lessons shared in her book, have instilled in her a deep sense of peace and self-love.

To keep up with Giovanna's upcoming adventures and to stay informed about her future endeavors, follow her on Instagram at @ConfusedGirlLA and subscribe to her email list at www.confusedgirlinthecity.com.

Notes

1.   Leah Collins, "Job Unhappiness Is at a Staggering All-Time High, According to Gallup," CNBC, August 12, 2022, https://www.cnbc.com/2022/08/12/job-unhappiness-is-at-a-staggering-all-time-high-according-to-gallup.html.

2.   *Merriam-Webster Dictionary*, "ego," accessed September 16, 2024, https://www.merriam-webster.com/dictionary/ego.

3.   Ram Dass, quoted in Goodreads, accessed September 16, 2024, https://www.goodreads.com/quotes/891994-souls-love-that-s-what-souls-do-egos-don-t-but-souls.

4.   Allen Saunders, quoted in Canadian Foundation for Economic Education, "Module 3. Your Goals: Some Things to Consider," Money and Youth, accessed September 17, 2024, https://moneyandyouth.com/modules/your-goals-some-things-to-consider/.

5.   Charles Dickens, *Great Expectations*, vol. 1 (James G. Gregory, 1861), 220, https://www.google.com/books/edition/Great _Expectations/MQIwAAAAYAAJ?hl=en&gbpv=0.

6.   Ecclesiastes 3:1 (English Standard Version).

7.   E. J. Albertsen, L. E. O'Connor, and J. W. Berry, "Religion and Interpersonal Guilt: Variations Across Ethnicity and Spirituality," *Mental Health, Religion & Culture* 9, no. 1 (2006): 67–84, https://awspntest.apa.org/doi/10.1080/13694670500040484.

8.   Quoted in Crystal Martin, "Bradley Cooper *Is* That into You," *Redbook*, December 15, 2008, https://www.redbookmag.com/love-sex /mens-perspective/interviews/a4497/bradley-cooper-celeb-interview/.

9.   United States Conference of Catholic Bishops, *Catechism of the Catholic Church*, 2nd ed. (United States Conference of Catholic Bishops, 2019), 565, https://www.usccb.org/resources /catechism-cahtholic-church.

10. Iyanla Vanzant, *Forgiveness: 21 Days to Forgive Everyone for Everything* (Smiley, 2013), 215, https://books.google.com/books ?id=32H6DwAAQBAJ&printsec=copyright#v=onepage&q&f=false.

11. Jean M. Twenge, *Generations: The Real Differences Between Gen Z, Millennials, Gen X, Boomers, and Silents—and What They Mean for America's Future* (Simon & Schuster, 2023), 392, https://www.google .com/books/edition/Generations/UCS2EAAAQBAJ?hl=en&gbpv=0.

12. For more information, see Pete Dalton, "The Aloha Spirit Book:

A Simple Guide to the Huna Power of Blessing," Urban Huna, October 9, 2017, https://www.urbanhuna.org/aloha-spirit-booklet/.

13. Quoted in Hatem Alakeel, "From Harvard Alumni to Supporting Women in the Workspace: Meet HRH Al Joharah Bint Talal Al Saud a True Role Model for Entrepreneurs & Beyond!" Gems of Arabia, accessed September 11, 2024, https://authenticite.me/gems-of-arabia/hrh-al-joharah-bint-talal-al-saud/.

14. Kurt Vonnegut, *A Man Without a Country* (Seven Stories Press, 2005), 24, https://books.google.com/books?id=T7J-Xg2bYKAC&vq=no+matter+how+well&source=gbs_navlinks_s.

15. Cher-Yi Tan et al., "Being Creative Makes You Happier: The Positive Effect of Creativity on Subjective Well-Being," *International Journal of Environmental Research and Public Health* 18, no. 14 (July 6, 2021), https://www.ncbi.nlm.nih.gov/pmc/articles/PMC8305859/.

16. G. E. Swan and D. Carmelli, "Curiosity and Mortality in Aging Adults: A 5-Year Follow-Up of the Western Collaborative Group Study," *Psychology and Aging* 11, no. 3 (1996), https://psycnet.apa.org/record/1996-06396-007.

17. Jackie Mader, "Want Resilient and Well-Adjusted Kids? Let Them Play," The Hechinger Report, November 14, 2022, https://hechingerreport.org/want-resilient-and-well-adjusted-kids-let-them-play/.

18. Association for Psychological Science, "Tidy Desk or Messy Desk? Each Has Its Benefits," ScienceDaily, August 6, 2013, https://www.sciencedaily.com/releases/2013/08/130806091817.htm.

19. David H. Freedman, quoted in Brian Wise, "Neat vs. Messy: Which Is Better for Creativity," WQXR, March 19, 2015, https://www.wqxr.org/story/neat-vs-messy-which-better-creativity/.

20. Jeffrey Borenstein, "Self-Love and What It Means," Brain & Behavior Research Foundation, February 12, 2020, https://bbrfoundation.org/blog/self-love-and-what-it-means.

21. Jaruwan Sakulku, "The Impostor Phenomenon," *International Journal of Behavioral Science* 6, no.1 (September 2011): 75–97, https://doi.org/10.14456/ijbs.2011.6.

22. Taylor Swift, quoted in Lewis Corner, "Taylor Swift Premieres New Single 'Begin Again' Music Video—Watch," Digital Spy, October 24, 2012, https://www.digitalspy.com/music/a432986/taylor-swift-premieres-new-single-begin-again-music-video-watch/.

23. Kristin Neff, "What Is Self-Compassion?" Self-Compassion, accessed September 16, 2024, https://self-compassion.org/what-is-self-compassion/.

24. Joe Vitale and Ihaleakala Hew Len, *Zero Limits: The Secret Hawaiian System for Wealth, Health, Peace, and More* (Wiley, 2010):175, https://books.google.com.bz/books?id=2UCWAAAAQBAJ&source=gbs_navlinks_s.

25. Groucho Marx, *100 Quotes by Groucho Marx*, narrated by Brad Carty (SAGA Egmont, 2022), https://www.audible.com/pd/100-Quotes-by-Groucho-Marx-Audiobook/B0BQ6WY491.

26. Sarah Rappaport, "The Global Wellness Industry Is Now Worth $5.6 Trillion," Bloomberg, November 9, 2023, https:// www.bloomberg.com/news/articles/2023-11-09/the-global -wellness-industry-is-now-worth-5-6-trillion.

27. Sleep Health Foundation, "Ten Tips for a Good Night's Sleep," January 12, 2024, https://www.sleephealthfoundation.org .au/sleep-topics/ten-tips-for-a-good-nights-sleep.

28. Alan Watts, quoted in Ganesh Das Braymiller, "Dancing with Change: Ram Dass x Alan Watts," Be Here Now Network, accessed September 17, 2024, https://beherenownetwork.com /dancing-with-change-ram-dass-x-alan-watts/.

29. Eckhart Tolle, *The Power of Now, A Guide to Spiritual Enlightenment* (New World Library, 2010): 30, https://www.google.com /books/edition/The_Power_of_Now/sQYqRCIhFAMC?hl =en&gbpv=0.

30. Robert Creenan, "Willow Labyrinth Opening New Indoor Labyrinth in the Thumb," *Manistee News Advocate*, May 4, 2022, https://www.manisteenews.com/news/article/Willow -Labyrinth-opening-new-indoor-labyrinth-17142604.php.

31. Albert Einstein, quoted in "Thoughts on the Business of Life," *Forbes*, accessed September 16, 2024, https://www.forbes.com /quotes/173/.

32. Good News Network, "70% Say They Always Trust Their Instinct, with Physical 'Gut Feeling' Used to Make Decisions,

Says New Poll," June 18, 2022, https://www.goodnewsnetwork
.org/70pt-say-they-always-trust-their-instinct-british-poll/.

33. Jo Hyunju et al., "Physiological Benefits of Viewing Nature: A
Systematic Review of Indoor Experiments," *International Journal
of Environmental Research and Public Health* 16, no. 23 (December
2019): 4739, https://www.ncbi.nlm.nih.gov/pmc/articles
/PMC6926748/; Jim Robbins, "Ecopsychology: How Immersion
in Nature Benefits Your Health," *Yale Environment 360*, January 9,
2020, https://e360.yale.edu/features/ecopsychology-how
-immersion-in-nature-benefits-your-health.

34. Judith Orloff, "The Neuroscience of Women's Intuition,"
Psychology Today, updated August 12, 2024, https://www
.psychologytoday.com/us/blog/the-genius-of-empathy/202406
/the-neuroscience-of-womens-intuition.

35. Michelle Martin, "Learning to Trust Your Women's Intuition,"
HuffPost, updated June 7, 2017, https://www.huffpost.com/entry
/womens-intuition_b_10192222.

36. Audrey Hepburn, quoted in Maggie Parker, "13 of Audrey
Hepburn's Most Inspiring Quotes," *Time*, May 4, 2016, https://
time.com/4316700/audrey-hepburn-inspiring-quotes/.

37. "Kindness Matters Guide," Mental Health Foundation,
accessed September 4, 2024, https://www.mentalhealth.org.uk
/explore-mental-health/kindness/kindness-matters-guide;
"The 6 Best Benefits of Helping Others You May Not Realize,"
The Midnight Mission, March 10, 2019, https://www.midnight

mission.org/the-6-best-benefits-of-helping-others-you-may-not
-realize/.

38. National Institute of Mental Health, "Major Depression,"
updated July 2023, https://www.nimh.nih.gov/health/statistics
/major-depression.

39. American Psychiatric Association, "What Is Depression?" April
2024, https://www.psychiatry.org/patients-families/depression
/what-is-depression.

40. American Psychological Association, "Overcoming
Depression: How Psychologists Help with Depressive Disorders,"
updated March 7, 2023, https://www.apa.org/topics/depression
/overcoming.

41. Roberta Ndlela, host, *Speaking and Communicating Podcast*,
podcast, episode 2 show notes, "2 Ears and 1 Mouth—
Use in Proportion!" October 23, 2021,
https://sac.bepodcast.network/2/transcript.

42. *Collins Dictionary*, "monk," accessed September 16, 2024,
https://www.collinsdictionary.com/dictionary/english/monk.

43. Greater Good Science Center, "Supporting Well-Being and
Building a Culture of Gratitude in Nursing," University of California, Berkeley, accessed September 10, 2024, https://ggsc.berkeley
.edu/gratitudefornurses.

44. Summer Allen, "The Science of Gratitude," Greater Good

Science Center, May 2018, https://ggsc.berkeley.edu /images/uploads/GGSC-JTF_White_Paper-Gratitude-FINAL.pdf.

45. "Health Benefits of Gratitude," UCLA Health, March 22, 2023, https://www.uclahealth.org/news/article /health-benefits-gratitude; Ernst T. Bohlmeijer, et al., "Promoting Gratitude as a Resource for Sustainable Mental Health: Results of a 3-Armed Randomized Controlled Trial up to 6 Months Follow-up," *Journal of Happiness Studies* 22 (May 7, 2020): 1011–1032, https://doi.org/10.1007 /s10902-020-00261-5.

46. Yoga Alliance, https://www.yogaalliance.org/.

47. Tanya Luhrmann, quoted in Sandra Feder, "Religious Faith Can Lead to Positive Mental Benefits, Writes Stanford Anthropologist," *Stanford Report*, November 13, 2020, https://news.stanford .edu/stories/2020/11/deep-faith-beneficial-health.

48. Oprah Winfrey, "20 Life-Affirming Quotes from Oprah Winfrey," Oprah.com, accessed September 5, 2024, https://www.oprah .com/inspiration/20-life-affirming-quotes-from-oprah-winfrey/all.

49. Angela Thoreson, "Helping People, Changing Lives: 3 Health Benefits of Volunteering," Mayo Clinic Health System, https: //www.mayoclinichealthsystem.org/hometown-health /speaking-of-health/3-health-benefits-of-volunteering.

50. VolunteerMatch, https://www.volunteermatch.org/.

51. Jack Feuer, "The Clutter Culture," *UCLA Magazine*, July 1, 2012, https://newsroom.ucla.edu/magazine/center -everyday-lives-families-suburban-america.

52. Amit Bhattacharjee and Cassie Mogilner, "Happiness from Ordinary and Extraordinary Experiences," *Journal of Consumer Research* 41, no. 1 (June 2014): 1–17, https://www.jstor.org /stable/10.1086/674724.

53. Bronnie Ware, *The Top Five Regrets of the Dying: A Life Trans-formed by the Dearly Departing* (Carlsbad, CA: Hay House LLC, 2012), https://books.google.com/books/about/The_Top_Five _Regrets_of_the_Dying.html?id=OL8ne9Zgf88C.

54. Eleanor Roosevelt, quoted in Michele W. Albion, ed., *The Quotable Eleanor Roosevelt* (University Press of Florida, 2013): 2105, https://www.google.com/books/edition/The_Quotable _Eleanor_Roosevelt/KX7SEAAAQBAJ?hl=en&gbpv=0.

55. Lao Tzu, quoted in Goodreads, accessed September 16, 2024, https://www.goodreads.com/quotes/34644-nature-does-not -hurry-yet-everything-is-accomplished.

56. Frances Gies and Joseph Gies, *Marriage and the Family in the Middle Ages* (Harper Perennial, 2019), https://books.google .com/books?id=ozthwwEACAAJ&printsec=frontcover&dq =editions:ISBN0062966812.

57. Barry Manilow, *Sweet Life: Adventures on the Way to Paradise* (McGraw-Hill: 1987): 264, https://books.google.com/books

?id=apdZAAAAYAAJ&focus=searchwithinvolume&q=nobody+is
+going+.

58. "Divorce Statistics: Over 115 Studies, Facts and Rates for
2024," Wilkinson & Finkbeiner, accessed September 16, 2024,
https://www.wf-lawyers.com/divorce-statistics-and-facts/.

59. Crystal Raypole and Tom Rush, "How to Recognize and Break
Traumatic Bonds," Healthline, updated June 12, 2023,
https://www.healthline.com/health/mental-health/trauma-bonding.

60. Joan E. Childs, "How Healing Your Inner Child Can Heal
Your Relationship," joanechilds.com, accessed September 9, 2024,
https://joanechilds.com/heal-your-inner-child-to-heal-your
-relationship/.

61. Jennifer Livingstone, "Don Miguel Ruiz's Four Agreements
and a Journey Towards Kindness," *The CuriousWorthy* (blog),
April 23, 2019, https://thecuriousworthy.com/2019/04/23/don
-miguel-ruizs-four-agreements-and-a-journey-towards-kindness/.

62. *Oxford English Dictionary*, "expectations," accessed September
16, 2024, https://www.oed.com/search/dictionary/?scope
=Entries&q=expectations.

63. *Merriam-Webster Dictionary*, "standard," accessed
September 9, 2024, https://unabridged.merriam-webster.com
/collegiate/standard.

64. Sharon Salzberg, *Real Love: The Art of Mindful Connection*

(Flatiron, 2017): 66–7, https://www.google.com/books/edition /Real_Love/WN58DQAAQBAJ?hl=en&gbpv=0.

65. Jack Beresford, "Little Girl's Reaction to Tragic Scene in 'Lion King' Has Viewers in Tears," *Newsweek*, September 29, 2022, https://www.newsweek.com/little-girl-reaction-tragic-lion -king-scene-tiktok-video-1747629.

66. Katty Kay and Claire Shipman, quoted in "Girls' Confidence Plummets Starting at Age 8: Here's How to Keep Her Confidence Strong," *A Might Girl* (blog), February 28, 2024, https://www .amightygirl.com/blog?p=27408.

67. Germaine Greer, quoted in Susan Ratcliffe, ed., *Little Oxford Dictionary of Quotes*, 5th ed., (Oxford University Press, 2012): 318, https://www.google.com/books/edition/Little_Oxford_Dictionary _of_Quotations/qZacAQAAQBAJ?hl=en&gbpv=0.

68. Jacqueline Ghosen, "Humility Key to Effective Leadership," *UB Reporter*, December 19, 2011, https://www.buffalo.edu /ubreporter/archive/2011_12_22/humble_leadership.html.